The Joyful Heart

Daily Meditations

Through the Year with
Watchman NEE

The Joyful Heart

Daily Meditations

Through the Year with
Watchman NEE

CLC
PUBLICATIONS
Fort Washington, PA 19034

The Joyful Heart:
Through the Year with Watchman Nee

U.S.A.
P.O. Box 1449, Fort Washington, PA 19034

GREAT BRITAIN
51 The Dean, Alresford, Hants. SO24 9BJ

This edition published in 2012
by CLC Publications
Fort Washington, Pennsylvania

Printed in the United States of America

ISBN-10 (mass market): 1-61958-042-X
ISBN-13 (mass market): 978-1-61958-042-8
ISBN-13 (e-book): 978-1-61958-057-2

JANUARY 1

"Forgetting the things which are behind, and stretching forward to the things which are before, I press on."
Philippians 3:13, 14

Because God acts in history, the flow of the Spirit is ever onward. We who are on earth today have inherited vast wealth through servants of Jesus Christ who have already made their contribution to the Church. We cannot overestimate the greatness of our heritage, nor can we be sufficiently grateful to God for it. But if today you try to be a Luther or a Wesley, you will miss your destiny. You will fall short of the purpose of God for this generation, for you will be moving backwards while the tide of the Spirit is flowing onwards. The whole trend of the Bible, from Genesis to Revelation, is a forward trend.

God's acts are ever new. To hold on to the past, wanting God to move as he has formerly done, is to risk finding yourself out of the mainstream of his goings. The flow of divine activity sweeps on from generation to generation, and in our own time it is still uninterrupted, still steadily progressive.

JANUARY 2

"I am the Alpha and the Omega, saith the Lord God."
Revelation 1:8

It is God who made the original design, and it is God who will bring it to completion. How can we thank Him enough that He is the Alpha, the initiator of all things? "In the beginning God . . ." When the heavens and the earth were created, it was God who purposed it all. All things had their origin in Him.

But at the same time He is the Omega. Man can and will fail; he may have good intentions and make fine promises, but they will always lack fulfillment. God, however, never gives up. He will never let any part of His purpose for mankind go unfulfilled. Do you doubt that? If the day should come when you feel that His work cannot be successful, listen to Him again as He affirms, "I am the Alpha and the Omega."

JANUARY 3

"Say not ye, There are yet four months, and then cometh the harvest?" John 4:35

The disciples were prepared to wait four months before tackling the task, but our Lord told them that the time to work is now, not at some future date. "Lift up your eyes and look . . . ," He said, indicating the kind of workmen He needed; that is, those who do not stand waiting for the work to come to them, but have eyes to see the work that is already waiting to be done.

Have you ever come across any "Go slow" workmen? They take in hand to do a piece of work, but they dawdle over it and drag it on and on as long as they can preserve any semblance of industry, for they are not seriously bent on working, but are really killing time. How unlike this was the Lord Jesus! "My Father worketh even until now," He declared, "and I work."

JANUARY 4

"Jesus said unto them, 'Verily, verily I say unto you,
Before Abraham was born, I am.'" John 8:58

The Gospel of John is the most profound of
all the Gospels, as well as being the last written. In it we are shown what is God's estimate of
Christ. So we are made to understand that it is
not a matter of God requiring a lamb, giving His
people bread, or providing us with a way, nor
even that Christ can use His power to restore
a dead man's life or a blind man's sight. In the
whole of this Gospel we are confronted with one
monumental fact: Christ is all these things.

He did not say that He is able to give people
light, but rather that He Himself is the Light of
the world. He did not only promise us the bread
of life, but assured us that He Himself is the
bread of life. He did not just say that He would
guide us in the way, but insisted that He Himself
is the Way. In Christianity Christ is everything.
What He gives is His very own Self.

JANUARY 5

*"If I have wrongfully exacted aught of any man,
I restore fourfold." Luke 19:8*

Zacchaeus sets us a good example. The power of the Lord was so greatly upon him that he was willing to restore fourfold all that he had gained by cheating. The principle in Leviticus was to add one fifth part only to the whole, but Zacchaeus was moved to do so much more.

His fourfold indemnity was not a condition for becoming a son of Abraham, nor was it a requirement for receiving the salvation of God. It was, however, the result of his being a son of Abraham and of having salvation come to his house. Moreover, by making restoration fourfold he effectively sealed the mouth of the critics of Jesus' actions of visiting him. His act played no part in securing his forgiveness by God. It did, however, have a definite bearing on his testimony before men.

JANUARY 6

"All things whatsoever ye pray and ask for, believe that ye receive them, and ye shall have them." Mark 11:24

We Christians often have a wrong concept of faith. The Lord says that he who believes that he has received shall receive, whereas we maintain that he who believes that he will receive shall have it.

Will you permit me to say something out of my own experience? It is that prayer may be divided into two parts. The first is praying without any promise until the promise is given. All prayers begin this way. The second is praying from the point at which the promise is given until it is realized and the promise is fulfilled. Faith is not just saying that God will hear you; it is coming to the place where, because God has promised, you can truthfully claim that He has already heard your prayer. So we may say that the first part is praying from no faith to faith; the second part is praying from faith to actual possession.

~

JANUARY 7

*"Comfort ye, comfort ye my people, saith your God.
Speak ye comfortably to Jerusalem." Isaiah 40:1, 2*

The previous chapter tells how all the values
of Isaiah's preaching and praying had been
thrown away by the foolish conceit of Hezekiah.
As a result of the king's display of all his treasures to the Babylonian ambassadors, Isaiah had
to speak the sad words of prophecy: "All . . . shall
be carried to Babylon; nothing shall be left."

A lesser man than Isaiah would have given
up in despair. All his life's work seemed to lie
in ruins. But the prophet's ministry was based
upon such a clear vision of the Lord of hosts
that he was able to continue with the new task
of comforting God's people and pointing them
on to restoration and recovery. Isaiah was a true
overcomer.

২

JANUARY 8

"Take us the foxes, the little foxes, that spoil the vineyards; for our vineyards are in blossom."
Song of Songs 2:15

What are these "little foxes" which are so destructive? Every small appearance of the old life—a habit, a bit of selfishness, uncrucified pride, a tendency to dwell on past grievances—all these and much more are the little foxes. These are not the grave sins, the shameful reversion to the world, but the unobtrusive and often unnoticed contradictions of our calling in Christ. How they spoil what might otherwise be such a delight to God! We are told that in one who has a reputation for wisdom and honor, even a little folly can give that which was fragrant an unpleasant odor.

Such follies and foibles threaten to prevent the vines whose blossom is so full of promise from ever realizing their capacity for fruitfulness. Now it might be thought that such minor failings could easily be dealt with, but evidently it is not so. The Beloved does not leave us to cope with them by ourselves. "Let us take . . . ," He whispers. "You need My help. We will do it together."

JANUARY 9

"When the sun was risen, they were scorched; and because they had no root, they withered away."
Matthew 13:6

The real trouble was not the sun, but the lack of roots. In the spiritual life roots represent that part of the life which has a secret history with the Lord. Those who live their lives only before men lack that secret history. May I ask you a straight question? What proportion of your life is lived in secret? Is any of it hidden from the eyes of man? Is your prayer-life limited to the prayers you utter in prayer meetings? Is your knowledge of the Word of God limited to what you preach? Are all your intimate spiritual experiences shared with other people? If so, then you lack roots.

It is those Christians who have a history with God in the secret place who triumphantly survive the fiery trials of the way. If one day we are faced with the option of renouncing our faith or losing our lives, which will we choose? It is not in that day that the issue will be settled; it is now. If in that day we fail Him, it will be because we have not sent down our roots deep enough today.

≈

JANUARY 10

"Shouldest not thou also have had mercy on thy fellow-servant, even as I had mercy on thee?" Matthew 18:33

We can find many things in the Bible which God does not like. One that He most dislikes is unwillingness to forgive on the part of his children. It is exceedingly ugly in the sight of God for the forgiven sinner to be merciless, and for the recipient of divine grace to be ungracious.

The Lord expects you to treat others as He has treated you. The servant in the parable may have been righteous in his demand for payment, but a Christian's relationships are based, not on being righteous, but on being also gracious. We must not remember another's sins, nor should we demand justice, for just though our demands may be, yet to do so is sinful. The basis for a believer's relations with others is never righteousness alone. It is the grace of God.

JANUARY 11

"Therefore will Jehovah wait, that he may be gracious unto you." Isaiah 30:18

God is a marvelous speaker. But a more arresting fact is this: God is a marvelous listener. In the book of Job thirty-five of the forty-two chapters record nothing but the discourses of several men. Throughout twenty-nine whole chapters Job and his three friends held forth; and all the while God silently listened. There was another listener too, a man called Elihu. He was a God-fearing man who exercised unusual restraint while the three tried to talk Job into silence and while Job in turn tried to silence them. At length Elihu could restrain himself no longer, and he broke out into an eloquent discourse which fills six more chapters of the book.

Elihu was a good listener, but his patience was limited. God alone could listen with unlimited patience. He listened silently to all that Job had to say, to all that his friends had to say, and to all that Elihu had to say as well. On and on they talked, and on and on God listened, until the four had exhausted themselves. God has amazing ability to listen—that in the end He may be gracious.

JANUARY 12

"As many as are led by the Spirit of God, these are sons of God." Romans 8:14

A Christian once appealed to his fellows, "Please ask God to show you what He wants me to do, and when He does, tell me what it is." We can understand his request but, all unintentionally, it was a violation of the New Testament. God makes no provision there for mediators between ourselves and Christ. We no longer look to men to tell us what we ought to do. The Lord, the indwelling Spirit, teaches us His will.

In Acts 21 we read that when Paul felt he should visit Jerusalem a number of people besought him not to do so because of the serious trouble which was expected to befall him there. Yet he declined to reverse his decision. Why? Because in his inner being he had assurance regarding the Lord's will. If we are truly walking with God, we dare not be governed by other people's opinions. In Old Testament times people might consult the prophets, but not so today.

JANUARY 13

"He ever liveth to make intercession for them."
Hebrews 7:25

How could the Lord ever have borne the burdens of others if He had been all the time thinking about His own great sufferings? But He did not. Instead He spent His days as though he had no burdens of His own, and gave Himself in sympathy as if He had nothing else to do. Nor was He sympathetic only to the people of His day; He is full of the same sympathy for us here and now. Often you may feel that nobody cares for you. At such times your burdens seem intolerable and earthly friends appear quite powerless to help and understand.

There is, however, a Friend who is always at hand to lift your heavy load. Though seated in the heavens, He seems to bend down and take you as His personal delight, and is deeply concerned with your welfare. He feels for you in your trouble and will fly to your support. Call on Him; He ever lives.

JANUARY 14

"If we confess our sins, he is faithful and righteous to forgive us our sins." 1 John 1:9

If a child of God should sin, and should continue in that sin without confession, he yet remains God's child. God is still his Father, but there is now a weakness in that believer's conscience: he is unable to be at ease with God. Though he may try to maintain fellowship with God, he will find fellowship both painful and limited. The spontaneity has gone. Within him there is an awareness of distance. But there is one sure way of immediate restoration and that is to go to God in confession of the sin, calling upon Jesus Christ as his Advocate to conduct his case.

Never let us linger, then, in the shame of sin, as if such self-inflicted suffering could itself work in us holiness. There is no merit in a sense of guilt that does not lead on to repentance. If any man sin, the one thing he must do is to go to God and confess, trusting in Jesus Christ the Righteous One to champion his cause.

JANUARY 15

"Behold, waters issued out from under the threshold of the house eastward." Ezekiel 47:1

The question is not whether the tide of the Spirit will flow on in our generation, but whether you and I will be caught up into that tide. We have a glorious heritage from the past, but we also have the solemn responsibility of passing it on. If we fail to fill our role in God's purpose for this present time, He will seek out others to do so. The fruit of the past has been possible because men of God stayed in the mainstream of His purpose. Now it is we who have the privilege of offering ourselves to Him that He may speed a little further on His course. If He can drive a way for himself through our lives, then that will be our greatest glory. If not, He will still go on, but will have to turn in some other direction, and we shall have the tragic experience of being bypassed.

It is not merely the proclamation of God's truth that is needed today; it is the release in human lives of the risen Christ to whom that truth points. This happens only as we ourselves are caught up in the Spirit's on-flowing tide.

JANUARY 16

"We know that to them that love God all things work together for good." Romans 8:28

Hangchow is a city of silk-weavers. Come with me into one of their sheds. Look at the reverse side of the brocade that is on the loom. To the untaught, the many-colored warp and woof seem only chaotic, a meaningless crossing of colored threads. But turn it over. Look at the front side of the finished fabric. It is beautiful, a tasteful design of men and trees, flowers and mountains. The work in progress was confusing, but the end product has meaning and purpose.

When our lot appears puzzling to our eyes, remember that we do not know to what design God is working. For each thread, bright or dark, has its function, and each change of pattern follows a prepared plan. What matter is it if life's experiences seem disorderly and we cannot grasp what they are all about? God's Word assures us that all things without exception work together for our good.

JANUARY 17

"We walk by faith, not by sight." 2 Corinthians 5:7

Forgive me for saying here something rather elementary about how God delivers us from living by our feelings and leads us into the state of living by faith. When you first find the Savior, you cannot but be happy. Everything is so wonderful, and everything is so new! But this feeling passes, and then what do you think? Because you are not as joyful as when you were first saved, have you lost your spirituality?

Certainly not! To think so is to display a serious misunderstanding of Christian experience. A simple illustration will help us. I lose a watch. When I find it, I am happy. When four or five days have elapsed, I am no longer as happy as I was. After a few more days, that happiness may have entirely gone. What has happened? My watch has not been lost again. All that I have lost is the feelings I had at the time of finding it. This is the Christian life.

JANUARY 18

"So teach us to number our days, that we may get us a heart of wisdom." Psalm 90:12

Reckoned on the calendar, the days we live are easily tallied up, since a day can be measured and so can a year. But reckoned according to God's valuation, some days are credited while others may be discounted. It appears that in the Bible some days go unrecorded, perhaps because God has looked upon them as wasted days, devoid of meaning for Him.

The day you receive the salvation of the Lord is the day you begin your spiritual history. Life, for you, starts then. Before that moment you really have no spiritual days to be credited in the time-scale of God. Even after you have believed in Him, it is not certain that each day or year necessarily counts. Tell me, have you never wasted a day?

Our calendar days are so few! How precious is every one! We need to learn how we can number them so that our every day and every year gives him pleasure.

JANUARY 19

"Ye shall have tribulation ten days." Revelation 2:10

What is the meaning of this "ten days"? When Abraham's servant wanted to carry off Rebecca, her brother and mother requested that she stay with them ten days. When Daniel and his friends would not allow themselves to be defiled by the king's food, they asked the officer in charge to try them for ten days. So the words must have a meaning in the Bible. It seems possible that they indicate "just a short time." Is this the Lord's meaning in His message to the church at Smyrna?

He seems to be saying, first, that there are certain days marked out for our suffering, and that those days are calculated by Him. They are inescapable, but after they are over we shall be freed. On the other hand, He seems to affirm that the trials are brief. The ten days are but a short time. No matter what tribulation you pass through before God, it will soon be past. Be faithful therefore. He awaits you with a crown of life.

꧁

JANUARY 20

*"And God said unto Jacob, Arise, go up to Bethel,
and dwell there: and make there an altar unto God."*
Genesis 35:1

Jacob was thinking of settling down peacefully in Shechem, but God could not approve. He permitted circumstances therefore—the humiliation of his daughter and the gross crime of his sons—that disturbed Jacob's peace and made it possible for God to speak to him again. At the time Jacob had no thought of God's hand in these events. Instead he blamed his sons and became frightened. Then he heard God's voice: "Arise, go up to Bethel."

I do not believe that a person can become so spiritual that he has no need to learn from his environment. Brothers and sisters, never consider yourselves so advanced in the Christian life that you need only listen to the inner voice. You may have become deaf to that! God then has to speak to you through what is going on around you.

JANUARY 21

*"How much more shall the blood of Christ . . . cleanse
your conscience from dead works to serve
the living God?" Hebrews 9:14*

The question of how the blood of Christ
cleanses our conscience cannot be resolved
in literal terms. Can we imagine some onlooker
at Calvary stepping forward and taking a little of
the blood of Jesus, touching it upon his body (as
was done symbolically with the Jewish offerings)
and so finding his conscience cleansed? No. For
us, the Holy Spirit deals not with symbols but
with spiritual realities.

When the Spirit cleanses our conscience by
appeal to the blood of Jesus, He is applying to
us the reality of the Lord's death on the cross.
Those who only live in the realm of symbols and
forms and rituals will find themselves bound by
conscience to dead works. The Spirit is life. He
works on the basis of the spiritual reality of the
shed blood to guide into a new and real relationship with the living God.

❧

JANUARY 22

"Pray to thy Father who is in secret, and thy Father
who seeth in secret shall recompense thee."
Matthew 6:6

All too often we lay stress on having prayer answered. Yet here the Lord Jesus emphasizes having prayer rewarded. How do we know this? Because the same word "recompense" used here is used again, with no petition implied, in verse 2 concerning alms and in verse 16 concerning fasting. Judged by its context, the recompense promised refers to a reward to be received in the future. What this tells us is that prayer answered is secondary, while prayer rewarded is primary. If our prayer is in accordance with the mind of God, it will not only be answered here. More important than that, it will be remembered in the future at the judgment seat of Christ, for reward.

Prayer is primarily communion with God for the manifesting of His glory. The hypocrites in this passage turn the things that should glorify God to the service of their own aggrandizement. They pray in public places for men to applaud—and love it. What is happening? They are praying merely to be seen by others, not to be heard by

God, and the motive determines the outcome. These people find their reward where they looked for it, in the praise of men. The recompense reserved in the kingdom to come, they miss altogether. They never really sought it.

❧

JANUARY 23

"And Jehovah said unto Joshua, Stretch out the javelin that is in thy hand toward Ai; for I will give it into thy hand." Joshua 8:18

The capture of big Jericho may have been a walkover, and here now is little Ai. Yet the means used successfully for the victory at Jericho cannot be applied here: something new is called for. In other words, you cannot tackle today's spiritual battles with yesterday's weapons. The past has become history and you thank God for it, but new power is needed now to deal with a new challenge.

To persist in self-reliance acquired through past successes is to close the door to progress. The Lord orders our circumstances to confront us with an ever-fresh need to seek His face, proving to us thereby that we can overcome every time by means of some new discovery of Him.

JANUARY 24

"Ye do err, not knowing the scriptures, nor the power of God." Matthew 22:29

When Herod asked the priests and scribes where the Christ should be born, they at once recited from memory the prophet's words: "In Bethlehem of Judea." How well they knew their Scriptures! They could give an immediate answer when called upon. And was their reply wrong? Not at all. Yet this was the surprising thing: that after they had answered the question, not one of those scribes or elders set out for Bethlehem. What they knew was quite accurate; nevertheless they only used it to point the way to the magi—and then went back to their books. They functioned like a traffic policeman who directs people to where they want to go, but he himself remains at his post.

This will not do. It is not enough just to know the Bible; we must also know the power of God. Understanding what He says in the Scriptures is not sufficient if it does not lead us to know God Himself. We need to have personal dealings with him, acting on His words in faith. The pathway to the knowledge of God is through such actions. There is no other way.

❧

JANUARY 25

"But thanks be unto God, who always leadeth us in triumph in Christ, and maketh manifest through us the savor of his knowledge in every place."
2 Corinthians 2:14

Fragrance is the world's most elusive commodity. The fragrance of a summer's day is impossible to define and you can't imitate it. This is also true in the spirit. Have you ever had the experience of sensing a special quality about a Christian man or woman which you could neither explain nor describe? That is what we mean by spiritual fragrance. It comes from a heart relationship with God which is born of communion and obedience, and it far surpasses all the cultivated excellencies of this world.

True, we may meet fine virtues in people who make no claim to be Christians, and at times these natural qualities put us, as mere men, to shame. But really there is no comparison. The fragrance which comes from a Spirit-directed life proceeds out of heaven itself. It originates from Christ, and it points men not to us but to Him.

JANUARY 26

"Be not ashamed therefore of the testimony of our Lord." 2 Timothy 1:8

Why should we be ashamed of confessing ourselves to be Christians? When the Lord Jesus was hanged on the cross, He bore our shame as well our sins. The Bible clearly teaches us that He was put to shame. He was humiliated by the soldiers in the Praetorium and disgraced by them at Calvary. If we suffer disgrace from men, that is our rightful portion; no indignity that we receive today can compare with the shame which our Lord endured on the cross.

Let it, then, be no surprise to us to suffer shame, for this is the portion of all who belong to the Lord. It is really the world which should be ashamed. A poet has exclaimed, "Can a flower be ashamed of the sun?" Impossible! As a flower opens gratefully for all to see its response to the sunlight, so will we openly confess before men the Lord who has done so much for us.

❧

JANUARY 27

"My heart is fixed, O God, my heart is fixed: I will sing, yea, I will sing praises." Psalm 57:7

Our problems in life are in general of two kinds. The first kind is circumstantial, arising from the turn of events. This may be met and overcome by prayer. The other kind is more personal, the suffering of being hurt or humiliated by others. For such affronts and misunderstandings prayer does not seem to avail. I myself have prayed, and I know. It is futile to wrestle with such problems and to strive in prayer about them. I want to suggest that you should turn instead to praise.

You should bow your head and say to the Lord, "Lord, I thank You. I receive this bad treatment as from Your hands and I praise You for it all." By so doing you will find that everything is transcended. What the Lord has permitted to come to you cannot be wrong. Everything that He does is perfect. As you thus praise God, your spirit rises victorious over your problems and God Himself takes care of your hurt feelings.

JANUARY 28

"Ye also, as living stones, are built up a spiritual house." 1 Peter 2:5

Solomon's Temple was built of quarried and trimmed stones, each stone in its place but every one lifeless. Today God's house is made up, not of dead, but of living stones. Peter, who wrote these words, was a living stone, a single unit, before he was built together with the others. Many remain thus, scattered here and there, independent, useless. But if a house is to be constructed they must be gathered, and stone must be built on stone and fitted to other stones.

Thank God you are His! You have trusted in the Lord Jesus, and now you are God's living stone. Don't, then, just hide out there alone in the shrubbery to become a cause of stumbling to the unwary! Let yourself be carried to the building site. Allow yourself to be matched up with other living stones, fashioned to fit into your place. The trimming may be uncomfortable, but in the end God will have a dwelling-place.

JANUARY 29

"Jesus, perceiving in himself that the power proceeding from him had gone forth . . . said, Who touched my garments?" Mark 5:30

In this story we are told that many thronged around the Lord Jesus, but only one touched Him. This woman came up behind Him in the crowd saying, "If I touch but His garments, I shall be made whole." She had faith and experience followed, for "she felt in her body that she was healed." And our Lord too felt the touch, and of course knew all that had transpired.

There was no change in the many who thronged around Him. It was solely the one who touched Him who was instantly changed. It is useless therefore merely to rub shoulders with the Lord. Too many today acquaint themselves with the externalities of Jesus of Nazareth without touching the Son of God as she did. They stay in the outside world of thronging and never venture into the inner world of touching. Do you see the difference? Merely to throng Him is of no avail. Reach out the trusting hand to touch Him, and diseases are healed and problems solved.

JANUARY 30

"Give us this day our daily bread." Matthew 6:11

Some may have trouble in understanding how the Lord can teach us to pray for God's name, God's kingdom, and God's will, and then suddenly turn to the matter of daily bread. It appears unfitting to take such a plunge in prayer from the sublime to the very mundane. But there is a good reason for our Lord's words. He knew only too well that those who are devoted to the will of God will become involved in fierce hostility; that those who pray kingdom prayers will inevitably draw upon themselves Satanic attacks which will threaten their very existence.

Bread is man's elemental need. If he is to stand for the will of God to be done on earth, he must be kept alive. Hence the relevancy of his asking for daily bread if he is to be true to God in this evil world.

~

JANUARY 31

"And a voice came out of the cloud, saying, This is my Son, my chosen: hear ye him." Luke 9:35

Christ is unique. Any comparison with Him is impertinent. Peter was so thrilled to see Moses and Elijah alongside his Lord that he proposed to make for them three tabernacles. But the divine voice effectively silenced him. Moses and Elijah were not to be counted on the same plane as Christ. Peter, of course, would doubtless have given Christ priority, relegating Moses and Elijah to second place and third; but God repudiated the idea that even a Moses or an Elijah, however prominent under the Old Covenant, should have authority in the New. Here "Christ is all and in all." Christianity is Christ—not Christ plus.

In effect God said, "This is no time for you to be talking; it is a time for you to be listening. Anything you or anyone else has to say is totally irrelevant. There is only One who is qualified to speak here." God's word today is not "Hear ye them," but "Hear ye him."

FEBRUARY 1

*"And they overcame him because of the blood of the
Lamb, and because of the word of their testimony."*
Revelation 12:11

When you see the significance of the blood
of Christ before God, you will have boldness before Him and a testimony before man.
Not only will you affirm confidently that sinners
can be forgiven and accepted because of Christ,
but you will further testify about God's kingdom. "Testimony" means telling others what
God has secured in Christ. It is a fact that Christ
is King; it is a fact that He is victorious and will
be so forever; it is a fact that He destroyed all the
works of Satan on the cross; and it is a fact that
the kingdom of heaven will come here upon this
earth.

Satan does not fear when we try to reason
with him, but he does fear when we proclaim
these facts concerning Christ. He does not mind
our knowledge of the Bible or our theology, but
he has to yield when, out of hearts committed to
Christ, we declare that Jesus Christ is Lord.

FEBRUARY 2

"Behold, I have given you authority . . . over all the power of the enemy: and nothing shall in any wise hurt you." Luke 10:19

Everyone who is called by the name of the Lord is, here on earth, his representative. We are God's ambassadors. Delivered out of the power of darkness and translated into the kingdom of His dear Son, we carry with us at all times the authority of heaven.

But a serious warning goes with this: that we ourselves must be subject to the authority of God. We know that the creation was originally placed under the control of man. Why, then, does the creation not listen to man's command today? Because man himself has failed to heed God's Word. Why did the lion slay the man of God from Judah (1 Kings 13:26)? Because he had disobeyed God's command. But on the other hand, how was it that the lions did not hurt Daniel? Because he was innocent before God. Or again, in the book of Acts worms consumed proud Herod, whereas a viper could not hurt the hand of Paul. Here at last the creation is once more subject to the ambassador of Christ. It all turns on the ambassador's own obedience.

FEBRUARY 3

"When I saw among the spoil a goodly Babylonish mantle, and two hundred shekels of silver, and a wedge of gold of fifty shekels weight, I coveted them, and took them." Joshua 7:21

The principle of Babylon is to pretend in order to receive glory from men. When Achan took the Babylonian garment, it could only be because he wanted to adorn himself, to outshine others. We find a similar sin in the New Testament when Ananias and Sapphira offended, by lying, to the Holy Spirit. Their devotion to the Lord was partial, but they wanted it to seem complete. They wanted to be looked upon by others as those who loved Him greatly. They were acting a part.

Here is a real danger to God's children—to pretend to be spiritual. Whenever in spiritual matters we put on a garment which does not match our actual condition, we are not being true worshipers but are following the principle of Babylon. The Father seeks those who, however simply, worship him in spirit and in reality.

FEBRUARY 4

"My soul shall make her boast in Jehovah." Psalm 34:2

We boldly claim that sin is beneath our feet, yet we tremblingly confess that as long as we live we may readily fall again. These contrasting experiences run parallel throughout the Scripture and are integral to our Christian life. The trouble is that we are apt to give our attention to only one of the two.

There are, on the one hand, some very strong, almost extreme words of confidence in Scripture: "God . . . always leadeth us in triumph," and "sin shall not have dominion over you." These are bold, boastful affirmations. Yet the same people who say these things also say with the utmost humility: "I am chief of sinners," and "If we say that we have no sin, we deceive ourselves." If these opposite statements are to be reconciled, then we must conclude that the two experiences together comprise the life of the Christian. We must know Christ's fullness, but we must also know our own corruption.

❧

FEBRUARY 5

"Look to yourselves, that ye lose not the things which we have wrought, but that ye receive a full reward."
2 John 8

It seems that at the end of the New Testament period, the enemy of souls found entry into the house of God and caused God's own people to turn aside from his ways. So John's ministry is not so much to lead further but to restore. John does not say anything startlingly new and original. All he does is to carry what has already been revealed to its consummation. What distinguishes him is his concern to bring the people of God back to a position they had lost.

The Lord's words about John were, "If I will that he tarry till I come, what is that to thee?" Till I come! The ministry of the Spirit of truth set forth by John will go on until the story is completed. The purpose of God in His Church is going to be accomplished, for nothing can thwart God. Let us learn from John, therefore, to be faithful until the Lord Jesus comes again.

୬

FEBRUARY 6

"What meaneth then this bleating of the sheep in mine ears?" 1 Samuel 15:14

The Spirit of the Lord departed from Saul because he did not follow out His explicit leading. Saul's pious protestation to Samuel that he had fulfilled the command of God shows how he tried to deceive himself. The phrase "utterly destroy" comes seven times in this chapter in regard to Amalek. God had made his meaning clear as could be. Saul, however, illustrates how the deceitful heart can argue its way out of the challenge of full obedience.

He did this first by yielding to his own judgment as to what was good or bad, rather than subjecting it to God's expressed verdict. Secondly, he did so in offering to put the matter right by making a sacrifice to God. For God is not to be bought off in that kind of way. There is no easy alternative to obedience to His expressed word—not even a sacrificial one. To obey is always better.

FEBRUARY 7

"And their eyes were opened, and they knew him."
Luke 24:31

Though the hearts of these two burned with warm appreciation of the truth about Christ, they had no inkling of how close and how intimate was their experience of Him personally. Like Mary, who had joyfully announced His resurrection to them before they set off on their journey, they completely failed to recognize Him when He drew near. Unlike her, however, they found nothing in His voice which enlightened them.

The Lord spent a lot of time with these two. All of it He occupied in the most profitable exercise of expounding the Scriptures. Yet still they did not know Him, though they must by then have been intellectually convinced that Jesus was the Christ and that He had risen from the dead. There are, however, two kinds of knowledge. One comes from study, the other from an inward seeing, and we need them both. Christianity is built on more than a Book: it is built on the spiritual revelation which comes with that Book.

☙

FEBRUARY 8

"Bring ye the whole tithe into the store-house ... and prove me now herewith." Malachi 3:10

The people of Israel were in deep poverty. If they had contemplated practicing this command, they would doubtless have protested that since their ten loads of rice were insufficient, how could nine loads possibly suffice? Since their ten bags of flour were not enough, how could they conceivably manage with nine bags? This is the foolish reasoning of natural man, and God reproved His people. He offered to open to them the very windows of heaven if only they would believe that the things impossible with men are possible with God.

May I tell you that having ten loads is the reason for your poverty, while nine loads could ensure your abundance. A man may reckon that the more he has in hand, the better is his financial condition. Such a man does not know that this is how his poverty came about. To bring to God is to enter into blessing; to retain in our hand may be to invite the curse of hunger.

꒰

FEBRUARY 9

"Jesus, knowing that the Father had given all things
into his hands, and that he came forth from God . . .
took a towel, and girded himself." John 13:3, 4

In Revelation 9 we read of a development
which, to the author of that book, lay far in
the future. "I saw a star from heaven fallen unto
the earth: and there was given to him the key
of the pit of the abyss. And he opened the pit
of the abyss; and there went up a smoke out of
the pit, as the smoke of a great furnace." This is
figurative language, but the falling star is obvi-
ously Satan, and we know that the bottomless
pit is his domain—his storehouse, we might say.
This suggests that the end-time is to be marked
by a special release of his powers, and men will
find themselves up against spiritual forces in a
new way.

The greatest need of the saints at such a time
is spiritual refreshment. The incident at the sup-
per declares that it was to refresh the disciples
that Jesus came forth from God. I think that in a
befouled world there is no greater power for God
today than to come forth from Him fresh with
the clean air of heaven.

FEBRUARY 10

"He that believeth on me, as the scripture hath said,
from within him shall flow rivers of living water."
John 7:38

If I am thirsty, I can come to the Lord Jesus and drink of Him. But if I meet others in need, I cannot pour out a cupful and hand it to them, but can only minister to their need as Christ is a spring of water in me. So I must keep on drinking if the needs of others are to be met through me.

This verse describes a true ministry of Christ that is open to us all. The Word of Christ, the living water, first enters our hearts and satisfies us. From there it wells up again to spread life around. The trouble is that the Word often ceases to live after it has passed through you and me. For it is not a matter of how many Scriptures we can quote to other people; rather it is the outflow from us of Christ indwelling. And for that we must be ever drinking of Him. No thirst will be quenched otherwise.

᙮

FEBRUARY 11

"Today is salvation come to this house." Luke 19:9

When God is at work, the camel passes through the needle's eye. In Luke 18 a camel came hesitantly to the needle's eye and failed to go through; but here at Jericho a camel passed right through.

How could Zacchaeus give as he did? Because that day salvation had come to him. He yielded, not because it was easy, nor because he had cried and prayed and then with a tremendous struggle given in. He did not surrender a bit today and a bit tomorrow until he was forced finally to surrender all. He who had hoarded for decades, risking many dangers and falling into great disrepute in order to build up his wealth, now let it all go—because God had brought salvation to his house.

FEBRUARY 12

"The riches of the glory of this mystery . . . is Christ in you, the hope of glory." Colossians 1:27

Frequently we listen to someone's account of an experience that has brought him blessing, and sense how precious it was, but we make the mistake of fixing our eyes on the event instead of seeing the Lord who brought it about. As a result, trying ourselves to reproduce the situation, we suffer only defeat. Let us be quite clear that trusting in the Lord Himself and following a formula are two totally different things. The testifying brother had, by the grace of God, known living contact with Christ, and as a consequence had found release and full satisfaction in God. We, however, attempting to imitate his methods, end up with an ineffectual copy of his experience.

Neither formula nor method works, but only the living Christ. The reason for many unanswered prayers and feeble Christian lives is found in the lack of this personal touch with the Lord. Merely to copy methods is not enough. Go to Him who is the only source of vital experience!

FEBRUARY 13

"The friends salute thee. Salute the friends by name."
3 John 14

Do you see that friendship is something very special? To be friends is a relationship which transcends rank or position. It is neither formal nor legal, but breaks through all barriers of status. Impossible as it must seem, a man may become the friend of God. Abraham did. If Abraham had acted only formally as a man, and if God acted formally as God, the two could never have become friends.

How rich in spirit was the aged Apostle John! Yet he had walked so far with God that when writing this letter, he did not speak of brothers and sisters but of friends. He who had arrived at the zenith of richness was so full of years that he could very well have patted the head of a sixty- or seventy-year-old and called him, "My child." But he did not do this. Seniority was forgotten, and instead he addressed him as "My friend." Someday, when you are very mature, you may make little children your friends!

FEBRUARY 14

"All these things are against me." Genesis 42:36

We must not imagine that Jacob no longer needed God's discipline after Peniel. He did, and he got it. From the time that Deborah, Rebekah's nurse, died, he experienced all sorts of family troubles. His beloved Rachel was taken from him. Simeon and Levi made the family name stink. Reuben, his eldest son, grievously wronged him. Then Joseph also disappeared, and Jacob had every reason to think he was dead and anticipated that he would go down to the grave mourning for this dear son of his. Only little Benjamin had been left to him, but now the time came when Benjamin, his last treasure, had to go. Everything seemed to be against him.

In fact, Jacob was just about to enter into his brightest period. His last days were not days of decline, but compare quite favorably with those of Peter and Paul and John. In some ways Abraham and Isaac faded away, whereas Jacob became quietly, blessedly fruitful.

FEBRUARY 15

"Praying at all seasons in the Spirit, and watching thereunto in all perseverance." Ephesians 6:18

New believers should take prayer seriously as a job to be done, and should prepare for themselves a "prayer book," a book of prayer accounts. Thus they will know how many things they have asked of God, how many times God has answered their prayers, and how many prayers are waiting to be heard.

Before any details are listed, several major matters should be recorded in the book to be prayed over daily: (1) All children of God should pray daily for the people of the world that they may be saved. (2) God's children should pray for the full restoration of Israel, for they are His chosen people. (3) Believers should ask the Head of the Church to give light, grace, and spiritual gifts to His own. How the Church today needs these things! And (4) Christians ought to pray for their countries, that they may lead a tranquil and quiet life in all godliness. Let us never overlook these oft-forgotten prayers.

✍

FEBRUARY 16

"And there was opened the temple of God that is in heaven; and there was seen in his temple the ark of his covenant." Revelation 11:19

God originally told the Israelites to make an ark or chest of shittim wood according to the pattern given to Moses in the Mount, and to place it in the Tabernacle. Later, when Solomon had built the Temple, the ark was transferred there. At length, with Israel captive in Babylon, the ark of God was lost. The symbol disappeared; but the reality it foreshadowed remains, for in heaven at the end, God again shows us the ark. What was that reality?

The ark was an expression of God Himself. It was reserved, not for man, but for God. By this sight of the ark in heaven we are assured that God will not deny Himself. He cannot revoke his pledges nor contravene his character. From it we must learn that what is of God can never fail, never be frustrated. By this glimpse into heaven God assures us that for His own name's sake, He will accomplish in the end all things that He has set Himself to do.

FEBRUARY 17

"And the Lord of that servant, being moved with
compassion, released him, and forgave him the debt."
Matthew 18:27

Do you see that this pardon illustrates the gospel? How absurd for the servant to plead for time when the proceeds from selling all that he had, and even selling himself, could not possibly repay the debt. It was as though he were saying, "Give me time. My intention is good. I am not thinking of evading my debt. I will do my best. I will pay back sometime in the future."

If we go thus to the Lord, He does not answer, "All right. Pay what you can now and clear up the rest of the debt bit by bit in the days to come." No, He freely forgives all. God gives grace and will go on giving until His own heart is satisfied. If He gives, He gives according to His own nature. We may ask boldly, for He always does abundantly above all that we ask or think.

FEBRUARY 18

"Besides me there is no God: I will gird thee, though thou hast not known me." Isaiah 45:5

In this passage we have a very peculiar thing. Cyrus, conqueror of Babylon and king of Persia, did not know God; yet he is described in these verses as the Lord's anointed. In the Scriptures, anointing always marks a man as chosen by God for His own special purpose, to fulfill a task for Him.

Cyrus is, then, an illustration for us of how world governments stand in the sight of God. He had no personal relationship with God. Yet he was in God's hand for the fulfilling of God's will. All such world powers are in God's hand. This one rises, that one falls, and God is over all. Of Cyrus God did not just say, "My instrument," but "My anointed." The rise and fall of nations in history is controlled by His sovereign choice for purposes that are only wise and good.

꩜

"For lo, the kingdom of God is within [margin: in the midst of) you." Luke 17:21

What did Jesus mean when He said these words to the Pharisees? He simply meant: "I am standing here." We all know that the kingdom of God could not be "within" the Pharisees, but on that day the kingdom was in their midst because its King stood among them. The presence of the Lord Jesus implies the unfettered rule of God. Where He is, the kingdom is.

Redemption has made us, too, into a kingdom (Revelation 1:6). Not only where the Lord Jesus is, but where His Church is, there is also the kingdom of God. This is the place where He is free to exercise His authority. He must have a sphere, provided here by us, for His kingdom, His power, and His glory to have free course. For us the important thing is not our future reward or supposed position in the kingdom; it is our fulfillment of the Church's role of bringing His kingdom down among men in the earth today.

FEBRUARY 20

"And I said, What shall I do Lord? And the Lord said unto me, Arise, and go into Damascus." Acts 22:10

Before he encountered the sovereign rule of God, Paul had taken upon himself to wipe out the Church; but after he had fallen to the ground and acknowledged Jesus as Lord, he was a changed man, able now to submit to directions from one of its members, Ananias of Damascus. In that moment when he was saved, Paul had come to know God's rule as well as his mercy.

How could Paul, a man of such dominating character, listen to the words of Ananias, an unknown Christian whom Scripture mentions only in connection with this incident? Clearly it was because he had now become subject to God's reign. Had he not encountered divine authority on the Damascus Road, he would never have become subject to an obscure Christian brother in that city.

FEBRUARY 21

"Love suffereth long, and is kind." 1 Corinthians 13:4

Paul knew only too well how easy it is to let loose, as from tinkling cymbals, a torrent of empty words. His own words were never empty, for he himself affirmed, "We believe, and therefore also we speak." It is quite easy to teach the truths about love which are found in this chapter, and perhaps even memorize the chapter to impress our hearers, but in the case of the writer we know that he wrote, not to impress, but from his heart.

The Corinthians had said many critical things about him. He talked a lot, but his words were unworthy of their notice. He wanted their money, but his own status was in question. He was not even a divinely commissioned apostle at all. And he was always vacillating: first he was coming to them, and then he wasn't. Paul listened to all these criticisms—and what did he do? He responded only with the kind and patient love of which he writes here so beautifully.

FEBRUARY 22

*"Give, and it shall be given unto you; good measure,
pressed down, shaken together, running over. . . ."*
Luke 6:38

God is willing to supply our needs, super abundantly if we will let Him. Never for a moment think that He is poor. The cattle upon a thousand hills are His; all things belong to Him. God is not one who cannot supply. He most assuredly can. But there is something we must do, a condition we must fulfill before we are supplied. What He requires is that we ourselves should give; then His promise follows that there shall be given to us again.

Christians should have a special way of managing their finances. The world calculates its income, but we Christians should measure revenue by outgoing. A meager income often follows inadequate giving. Proper giving almost guarantees a sufficient supply from God. If you do not give, then the Lord is under no obligation to give to you. Many have faith to ask God for money, but lack faith to give it away. When God gives, He always gives bountifully. He gives not only good measure, but pressed down, shaken together, and running over.

FEBRUARY 23

"Come and let us build up the wall of Jerusalem, that we be no more a reproach." Nehemiah 2:17

Separation to God, which means separation from the world, is a first principle of Christian living. If God wants His city with its measurements and its glory in eternity, then we must build in human hearts the wall which is the first feature of that city.

Nehemiah in his day succeeded in rebuilding the wall of Jerusalem, but only in the face of great opposition. For Satan hates distinctiveness; separation of men to God he cannot abide. Nehemiah and his colleagues armed themselves, therefore, and thus equipped for war they laid stone to stone. Let us follow their lead. Let us guard as precious all that is of God and be uncompromising in our separation unto Him. There is a reproach to be removed and we are called to build. This is a matter of first importance.

FEBRUARY 24

"Lay hold on the life eternal, whereunto thou wast called, and didst confess the good confession in the sight of many witnesses." 1 Timothy 6:12

We hold the view that a changed life without a corresponding oral confession is inadequate. Change in conduct is no substitute for confession with the mouth. I have frequently heard people say that if a man's conduct is good, he does not need to speak out for God. But such a position leaves him with a loophole. True, no one will speak against him if his conduct is good, but neither will they do so if his conduct is bad. If, however, he has openly confessed himself to be a Christian, then the moment he fails in behavior the world will rise up and charge him with inconsistency.

To insist on conduct without confession is to leave your back door open. By providing yourself with a way of escaping men's criticism if you fail in the matter of conduct, you have actually prepared for the day of failure. Close that loophole! Stand up and confess the Lord. Then, leaning on Him for help, live consistently with your confession.

FEBRUARY 25

"Jesus saith unto him, I am the way." John 14:6

God's way for man is not a route which can be charted on a map; indeed, it is not a thing at all, but a Person. His Son is the only means for attaining his end. The one and only way that leads from where we are to where God is, is Christ. All who have truly come to God have done so by making this discovery—that Christ does not merely teach us the way to the Father; He is the Way. We meet Him and He leads us to God. But going on from this first experience, we need to realize that progressively, no less than initially, we can approach the Father only through the Son. "I am the way" was true when we first came to God. It is still true and always will be.

Yet numbers of defeated Christians have for years sought what they would call the way of victory, and are still pursuing their weary quest. Alas, they are searching for a way and are missing him who is the Way. As long as we are trying to find some technique for overcoming sin and Satan, we are doomed to defeat. Formulae have their use in the world of nature, but in the realm of the spirit nothing has value apart from the living Christ Himself.

FEBRUARY 26

". . . though he was a Son, yet learned obedience by the things which he suffered." Hebrews 5:8

Inasmuch as rebellion came from created beings, so obedience must now be established among them. Man sinned by rebelling; therefore, the authority of God must be erected anew on man's obedience. This explains why the Lord Jesus came into the world and was made one with created men. He did so, and then broke the long tradition of human independence by walking humbly in the way of obedience to God. Please note that He did not merely bring obedience to the earth; he learned it in practice—and He did so through suffering.

We too may learn to practice obedience by the same means. Our usefulness is determined not by whether we have suffered, but by how much obedience we have learned as we walked with our Lord Jesus in that suffering. Those alone are useful to God who have learned, at whatever cost, to obey Him.

FEBRUARY 27

"Neither give place to the devil." Ephesians 4:27

Without some foothold in us, Satan cannot operate. Hence, his first tempting of us will be aimed at securing some ground; the next will be an assault from the ground he has secured. One very large territory, perhaps the largest, that he operates from is fear.

"Fear is Satan's calling card," a beloved counselor used to say to me. Whenever you accept his calling card, you will receive a visit from him. Fear him and he comes; fear not and he is held at a distance. No child of God need be fearful of Satan, even though he roar as a lion and his teeth are drawn. Within us is One who by demonstration is greater than he.

FEBRUARY 28

"And I, if I be lifted up from the earth, will draw all men unto myself." John 12:32

Over against the present world order, the Lord Jesus proclaims, "And I . . ." The expression contrasts sharply with what precedes it, even as the One it identifies stands in contrast with His antagonist, the prince of this world. Through the cross, through the obedience to death of Him who is God's grain of wheat (verse 24), this world's rule by compulsion and fear is to end with the fall of its proud ruler.

And with Christ's springing up once more to life, there has come into being in its place a new reign of righteousness and one that is marked by a free allegiance of men to Him. With cords of love their hearts will be drawn away from a world under judgment toward Jesus the Son of Man, who though lifted up to die was by that very act lifted up to reign.

FEBRUARY 29

"If we live by the Spirit, by the Spirit let us also walk."
Galatians 5:25

Walking after the Spirit implies that all our actions are to be subject to the Holy Spirit's own laws and principles. With these everything becomes sharply defined. There is a precise standard of right and wrong. What is right is right, whether the day is clear or cloudy. What is wrong is wrong, whether the matter is exciting or repulsive. The Christian's walk must follow a distinct standard.

The one who lives in his emotions will not be governed by principles but by the whim of vacillating feelings. Should he be thrilled, he may be tempted to undertake what he would ordinarily recognize as unreasonable. If, however, he feels despondent, he may not even perform what he well knows to be his duty. The law of the Spirit of life is God's remedy for this.

MARCH 1

*"When Christ, who is our life, shall be manifested,
then shall ye also with him be manifested in glory."*
Colossians 3:4

Many of us live in constant fear of temptation. We know just how much we can stand, but alas, we have not discovered how much Christ can stand. "I can stand temptation up to a point," we say, "but beyond that point, I am done for." If two children cry, the mother can stand it; but if more than two cry together, under she goes.

Yet it is not really a matter of whether two children cry or three. It is all a question of whether I am getting the victory or Christ. If it is I, then I can stand two only. If Christ, it won't matter if twenty cry at once! To be carried through by Christ is to be left afterwards wondering how it happened! This is a matter that God delights to bring us to with a new flash of understanding. Suddenly one day we see that Christ is our life. That day everything is changed.

MARCH 2

"Your Father knoweth that ye have need of these things." Luke 12:30

Many of us have experienced that again and again God has controlled us through money matters. When we have been in the center of His will, supplies have been sure; but as soon as we have been out of vital touch with Him, they have become uncertain.

In His own work God must have the sole direction. At times we have fancied God would have us do a certain thing, but He has showed us it was not His will by withholding the financial means to do it. So we have been held under the constant direction of the Lord, and such direction is most precious. If we ceased to be dependent on Him, how could such trust be developed? Our living by faith must be absolutely real. We must keep our eyes fixed on the unchanging God whose grace and faithfulness continue forever.

MARCH 3

"It is no longer I that live, but Christ liveth in me."
Galatians 2:20

God has not constituted Christ our Example to be copied. He is not giving us His strength to help us imitate Christ. He has not even planted Christ within us to help us to be Christlike. Galatians 2:20 is not our standard for record-breaking endeavor. It is not a high aim to be aspired to through long seeking and patient progress. No, it is not God's aim at all, but God's method.

When Paul says, "Christ liveth in me," he is showing us the life that gives God satisfaction in the believer, and there is no substitute. "Not I, but Christ" means Christ instead of me. When Paul uses these words, he is not claiming to have attained something his readers have not yet reached to. He is defining the Christian life. The Christian life is the Christ-life. God gives Christ to become my life and to live His life in me.

MARCH 4

"The prince of the world cometh: and he hath nothing in me." John 14:30

When man was tempted and fell, God cursed the tempter. "Upon thy belly shalt thou go," he said, "and dust shalt thou eat." The sphere thus allocated to Satan was the earth, and his food was to be the very substance of which man had been made. Satan had gained a clear title to all that man had become by turning from God. He has acquired "squatter's rights" in the old creation.

Praise be to God that, through Christ, Satan has now no rights in us. God the Redeemer met the situation by taking the old creation out of the way at Calvary and providing in Christ a new creation. So God has His Man. There is a Man who, even while He was on the earth, could affirm that the prince of this world had no claims upon Him whatever. And this Man is now on the throne, guaranteeing that Satan has no claims upon us either, since we have been redeemed. The Son of Man was glorified so that we, the many sons, may also be brought to glory.

≈

MARCH 5

"And Jehovah had respect unto Abel and to his offering." Genesis 4:4

Cain was a farmer and cultivated the soil. That was what his father had done in Eden. When Adam tilled the land there, we may conclude that he brought the produce of the earth and offered it to God. But now Cain was outside the garden of Eden because of sin. Nevertheless he tilled the soil as before, he received the produce as before, and he offered it to God as before. God not only refused to accept his offering, but also rejected him.

What man did before he sinned was acceptable to God, but nothing can be worse in God's eyes than for man to do the former things as though he had not sinned. Cain was just like this. He continued to offer things to God as though nothing had happened. To commit sin is bad enough, but not to be conscious of it is more serious. Abel, however, was accepted because he acknowledged that a change had taken place. His offering admitted that he had sinned and that the shedding of blood was needed to satisfy God.

MARCH 6

"He that sweareth to his own hurt, and changeth not."
Psalm 15:4

Whatever the nature of the contract, when the word of a Christian has been given, the promise must be honored. Because God keeps His word we have salvation; He is true to His pledge. The Gibeonites craftily deceived Joshua, and he made peace with them before discovering their plot (Joshua 9:19). Nevertheless, God insisted that the terms of the covenant be honored, and later withheld rain because King Saul went back on that undertaking.

God will not permit us carelessly to destroy a covenant. He who insisted that Joshua should spare the Gibeonites, and later that King David should avenge the wrong done to them, expects us to be true to our word, even if it be to our own disadvantage.

MARCH 7

"A good conscience; which some having thrust from them made shipwreck concerning the faith." 1 Timothy 1:19

A ship which is wrecked cannot sail. Whether a Christian can proceed with his service for God depends therefore on whether he has any offense outstanding on his conscience. Confession to God will remove the offense; but as long as the believer accepts the accusation of Satan, his conscience is stuck with it. He cannot effectively serve God until his conscience is at rest once again.

How wrong we are to believe in the devil's accusations more than we believe in the precious blood! When we commit sin we dishonor God; but when thereafter we fail to put our trust in the death of Christ for our sins, we dishonor Him even more. It is a shameful thing to sin, but it is more shameful still to look elsewhere for peace. If we have sinned and do not go to God about it, then we deserve to be accused. If we have confessed our sin, then what more can be said against us?

༒

MARCH 8

"Wherefore criest thou unto me? speak unto the children of Israel, that they go forward." Exodus 14:15

Paul prayed three times, asking the Lord to remove the thorn from his flesh, but was told, "My grace is sufficient for thee." Did he then pray a fourth time? No. Once the Lord had spoken, the issue was settled by His word.

If you pray after having received the promise, you will reintroduce doubt. Since God has already given you a word and you are in possession of faith, you ought instead to praise. If you continue to pray, you will merely dissipate your faith. To pray on is to pray out faith and give place to doubt. By doing so, you show that you do not believe what God has already told you. Even in human relationships, you will certainly ask if you have received no promise; but once the promise is given, do you not then give thanks?

MARCH 9

"And the light shineth in the darkness; and the darkness apprehended it not." John 1:5

There is a great danger today of concentrating attention on questions of dark things and making them the subject of conversation. We invite darkness by discussing it, seeking to deal with it, or even thinking about it. The Christian must learn in this to set aside everything that is negative and be occupied with the positive.

Darkness cannot be driven out of the world, but light can swallow it up. The reverse is never true. There is no such thing as darkness swallowing up light. Light is light wherever it is, even under a bushel. Let me repeat: here even in this dark world, light is light. All the world's darkness cannot extinguish it, but must itself retreat before even the glow of a tiny candle. When you meet darkness, it is absurd to dispel it. Just bring in the light.

MARCH 10

"Because I live, ye shall live also." John 14:19

God has given to us His Son to be to us our life as well as our substitute on the cross. To understand this, we must first be clear on what life is. When someone who is difficult calls on you, you know at once that the situation requires you to be patient, but whence does your patience originate? To supply it, you know you must draw from your very life. Often to be patient you must call forth the very best that is in you. You know this all too well.

Or let us suppose you have a big task ahead, and you feel you should be diligent and not slothful. To be diligent, too, calls you to put forth all your energies. Or again, someone is in trouble and you know you should show him love and helpfulness. But where does your power to help come from? It is your life, your nature, that causes you to love. The drain upon you is immense, as again and again you exercise your very life to meet outside demands. And here is the wonderful thing: God has given us Christ, with the purpose that He should be to you your life.

MARCH 11

"But Jesus saith unto him, Follow me; and leave the dead to bury their own dead." Matthew 8:22

Here is an unbelieving father who is still living, and a son who thinks it would be better to go home and wait for his father's death and burial before he begins to follow the Lord. Jesus counters this idea with the principle of letting the dead bury their dead. The "dead" here can only mean the spiritually dead, and by his words the Lord beckons the disciple to come away and leave burials to such people.

This in no way suggests that, for example, a new Chinese believer should not perform filial duties to his parents. Least of all should he be unmindful of their spiritual needs as they go to meet their God. What it stresses, rather, is the principle of letting the people of this world continue on with their unfinished business. Let us not wait until every earthly affair has been taken care of before coming to Christ. If we do, we may not have the time left to be Christians after all.

MARCH 12

"The river of God is full of water." Psalm 65:9

A tide has ebb and flow. Can God's life and power in the Spirit be characterized by like phenomena? By no means! His life knows no ebb, but is forever flowing. It does not rise and fall as the ocean, but is like a river, always full and strong. The tide must ebb at a certain hour. In the Source of the living water, there is no such "variation or shadow due to change."

If the fountain of life within the believer ever becomes restrained and ceases to flow, it is not because there is anything wrong with the inlet; it is the outlet which has become obstructed. The water of life must have a way through. It must go somewhere. Others must enjoy it. The answer is simple: first clear the outlet and it will flow again unceasingly.

MARCH 13

"In that same hour he rejoiced in the Holy Spirit."
Luke 10:21

We read only once in the Gospels about the Lord Jesus rejoicing, so it should be easy for us to learn something from this passage. It seemed as though He had failed in His ministry to these cities of Galilee, and yet He rejoiced in spirit. His joy clearly had nothing to do with circumstances, but was only gladness that the Father was doing what seemed good to Him. He rejoiced, not in the conscious success of His own work, but just in the will of the Father.

We are told that the joy of the Lord is our strength. It is this joy which upholds us; not that we have to seek to be joyful in imitation of Jesus, but that the very joy which he had is to be ours also. Of course in this life things around us will still cause us sadness, but is it not true that if we lose our joy we lose our strength? We must learn to live by His joy, which means rejoicing in our Father's good pleasure.

MARCH 14

"Christ Jesus came into the world to save sinners; of whom I am chief." 1 Timothy 1:15

This Paul, who fought the good fight, finished his course, and kept the faith, called himself the chief of sinners. The words "I am" are in the present tense. This reveals his own unchanging appraisal of himself. He had nothing to boast of. Like all the other sinners to whom he testified, he depended entirely on the grace of God.

More than that! He considered himself worse than the rest, feeling that he was in greater need of God's grace than anybody else. We may rightly consider him as a man who surpassed all others in having received light from the Lord. Possibly this very fact made him judge himself the more severely. It is the one who lacks divine illumination of himself who imagines he is advancing in holiness. He who has glimpsed the blaze of God's light has seen himself, too, as he really is.

ഛ

MARCH 15

"No man ever hated his own flesh; but nourisheth and cherisheth it, even as Christ also the church." Ephesians 5:29

We are told in verse 25 of this paragraph that Christ loved the Church and gave himself up for her. The verbs in the past tense point to the purpose of His death, that He might obtain for Himself a bride. Although her presentation to Him lies in the future, yet His work has already been finished in the past.

In our verse above, however, the verbs are in the present tense. The Lord is at present nourishing and cherishing His Church. The point is made that no man will hate his own flesh. If a normal person has hurt his hand, he carefully cherishes that hand; if his foot is injured, he tenderly cares for it. Knowing our care for ourselves, we can the better grasp how it is that Christ is now engaged in nourishing and cherishing us. We are parts of his Body, the cherished objects of His loving care.

MARCH 16

"The Lord Jehovah hath given me the tongue of them that are taught." Isaiah 50:4

These words are written prophetically about the Lord Jesus. They can be rendered, "the tongue of a disciple"; one, that is, who has disciplined himself to learn. The secret of spiritual advance is openness to be taught by God. We must throw heart and mind and spirit wide open to Him, preserving always a way for divine impressions to reach us. When in our youth we first engaged in Christian work, we fancied we knew all there was to be known, and were so set in our ideas that friends found it almost impossible to get anything different across to us.

Unteachableness is a barrier to progress. If a person cannot learn, what possibility has he of advance? Oh, may God deliver us from our reluctance to accept instruction! To receive through whatever means, humbly and without hesitation, whatever He desires to teach us is to prosper in the school of Christ.

MARCH 17

"O Lord, open thou my lips; and my mouth shall show forth thy praise." Psalm 51:15

A hymn should contain sound truth, poetic form and structure, and a touch too of divine inspiration. In this psalm, which tells of David's repentance, the truth is right and the psalm is poetically constructed. Moreover, in reading it we are aware of the depth of David's repentance, for it touches spiritual reality. Hence it draws forth a response from our spirits.

One basic requirement for any creative work for God is that it must command such a response in us. It must bring us into touch with divine reality. A hymn on consecration should excite in us a desire to consecrate ourselves to God. A hymn of worship should stir the heart to adoration. A hymn of thanksgiving should give words to our gratitude. David lived a real life. When he was happy, he leaped for joy. When he was sad, he wept. And when he was forgiven, his lips were opened to show forth the praise of God.

MARCH 18

"Be ye doers of the word, and not hearers only."
James 1:22

In the book of the Acts we find relatively little preaching. Its narrative is preeminently concerned with the works the apostles performed under the leading of the Holy Spirit. We discover what Peter was like, and that is the Word of God. We see also what Paul did, and again it is God's Word. We read about the beginning of the church in Jerusalem, in Samaria, in Antioch and elsewhere, and these are not merely historical records, but the Word of God as well.

Men speak out God's Word in history, but they work it out in history too, as the Holy Spirit reveals it through their lives. Thus the Word of God is full of the human element. Such is the peculiar feature of the Bible. The Bible is not a collection of devotional articles; it is men performing or living out the Word of God.

MARCH 19

"Be ye angry, and sin not: let not the sun go down upon your wrath." Ephesians 4:26

Of course to get angry and sin is always wrong; but how many of us think that the only way to avoid sinning is not to get angry! We simply do not know how to get angry and yet not sin. When Jesus cleansed the Temple, it was said of Him, "The zeal of thy house hath eaten me up." He was stirred with indignation. But alas, how few Christians know that Spirit-controlled stirring within that the Lord knew and consequently, how few know the spiritual authority that accompanied it!

There are many things in the world which ought to be rebuked, but how many really know how to administer that rebuke? We have lost the power. To slap a man on the shoulder when he is wrong, turning a blind eye to his deeds for the sake of friendship, is a cheap way out, whereas to rebuke him patiently and in love may be costly.

MARCH 20

"Ye shall be to me sons and daughters, saith the Lord Almighty." 2 Corinthians 6:18

Since there is neither male nor female in Christ, it may be surprising to encounter this distinctive reference to God's daughters. Perhaps the reason is that the verse refers to a very close personal relationship which is the comforting experience of those who are truly separated to God.

In church government male and female have their respective positions, but in the spiritual realm there can be no peculiar position for either, since Christ is all and in all. But in this highly personal matter of following the Lord and perhaps suffering for his sake, there is a special comfort for any Christian woman to know that she is a beloved daughter of her heavenly Father.

MARCH 21

"I have seen God face to face, and my life is preserved."
Genesis 32:30

God uses his light to expose to us our true situation. This is what brings us to our knees. As He did with Jacob at Peniel, God in mercy must bring us there, where we see what is the true spring and motive of our life. For remember, God is dealing with what we really are by nature. There, in the light of God, we must be as we are; we cannot pretend. Pretense is not Christianity. We may very much want to be different, but what we are by nature, we are. Nothing hinders God more than pretending it is otherwise.

The more "humble" some people are, the more one wishes they would show a little pride, because that would give God a chance to get on with the work. For it is never our pretense, but only God's touch that brings about transformation. If the work is to be done by me, it will get me nowhere. From being "natural" I shall merely become unnatural. But if the work is God's work, the changes wrought by Him have a definite purpose and direction. He starts with a Jacob and ends with an Israel.

MARCH 22

*"Ye that are Jehovah's remembrancers, take ye no rest,
and give him no rest, till he . . . make Jerusalem a
praise in the earth." Isaiah 62:6, 7*

When the children of Israel commenced to plan for their exodus from Egypt, the re-action of Pharaoh was to double their labor so that they had no time even to think about it. When you begin to plan or practice a more effective prayer life, Satan will counter by making you busier than ever with needs and responsibilities, so that you have no time for prayer.

You must not neglect your duties nor fail to take your responsibilities seriously, but you should put prayer first. In this realm the principle of tithing may also be helpful. After you have given God a tenth, you will discover that you can more efficiently use the remaining nine-tenths of your time. Give God His rightful portion and it may even be that the other nine-tenths is more effective than the ten tenths which you had before you tithed.

MARCH 23

"And the spirits of the prophets are subject to the prophets." 1 Corinthians 14:32

Suppose a musician is capable of playing three instruments, the piano, the organ, and the violin, with equal accomplishment. He may perform the same piece of music on each of them in turn, and since the three instruments possesses each its own distinct character, each performance will be a different work of art. The artist and music are the same, but each instrument in turn will provide its own unique flavor and color and feel.

The Lord's servants in the New Testament somewhat resemble these musical instruments. The same Gospel of Jesus Christ is preached through the pen of four different evangelists, giving us a picture of Him in four dimensions. How this enriches our understanding of Him! Under the government of the Holy Spirit, this personal element of each, far from clouding our view of God's living Word, enhances and interprets it all the more wonderfully. Is it surprising, then, that each of us, reading the Bible, encounters Christ in terms that match His own situation?

MARCH 24

"And the king was much moved, and went up to the chamber over the gate, and wept." 2 Samuel 18:33

Although Absalom was a rebel, he was still a son. When Saul died at the Philistines' hands, David mourned the death of one who had been his lawful king; but when Absalom was slain by Joab, David was inconsolable, though now it was a traitor that he mourned. The battle had been fought, treason had to be punished; yet David's father-heart was filled with sorrow at his son's death. Judgment had been necessary, but the tears flowed.

Judgment that is unmixed with tears discloses in us a grave deficiency of Christian love. If there is condemnation but no distress, then there is a sad lack in the family of God. It is wrong to condone evil, but it is even worse to harbor a vindictive spirit against the wrongdoer. We are told rather to forgive every one his brother from our hearts.

MARCH 25

"That I may know him, and the power of his resurrection." Philippians 3:10

When the Lord Jesus was here on earth, people knew Him in a variety of ways. Some had received things from His hand, some had leaned on His bosom, some had touched the border of His garment, and some had had their feet washed by Him. There were even those who, knowing Him already before His public ministry, might tell how He advanced in wisdom and stature in those thirty years. It was all very local and close at hand.

Today Jesus is risen, and we know Him by the Holy Spirit. The Lord has now become what those who touched him, or were touched by him, could not at that time have known. For today we meet the Lord of resurrection, the One who transcends all boundaries. The Church has continued on for nearly 2,000 years because there are always people who see the Lord of resurrection.

MARCH 26

"Though he slay me, yet will I wait for him." Job 13:15

What God expects of us is that we will not make personal enjoyment the purpose of our lives. As we run the spiritual race, we are to carry on whether or not we feel comfortable. Feelings and emotions are not to influence our attitude toward God. The life of faith is a life lived believing God under all circumstances.

It is always possible for us to know in our hearts that a certain course is God's will for us, yet to feel no enthusiasm for it. We may even feel dry and parched in spirit when we perform it. Worse still, the sense of the Lord's pleasure and the conscious experience of his blessing may be absent. It is as though we are passing through a dark ravine with the enemy contesting our way. Emotion begins to doubt when it enters such a valley of shadow, but faith trusts God and obeys even in the face of death.

MARCH 27

"And for this cause God sendeth them a working of error, that they should believe a lie." 2 Thessalonians 2:11

This world is unreal. Rejection of the truth has produced a state of affairs in which men are so deceived that they are confident that they are right. The deliberate liar cannot bear to be questioned, but the blinded do not mind because their deception has become the truth to them.

It is terrible to believe a lie. To believe the lies of others is bad enough, but it is much worse to believe one's own lies. Thank God for His illumination which can quickly dispel all such darkness. We need never fear deception if we maintain "the love of the truth" (verse 10) by which men are saved. The one great mistake is to avoid God's light, so closing our minds to Him who is the Truth.

"But we all, with unveiled face beholding as in a mirror the glory of the Lord, are transformed into the same image from glory to glory, even as from the Lord the Spirit." 2 Corinthians 3:18

Not only does the Spirit of God indwell regenerate man; He is ceaselessly at work refashioning him according to the image of Christ. We are wrong to treat the Holy Spirit merely as an honored guest when in fact He has been living in his house for ten or twenty years. He is the active owner-occupier, fashioning, building, reshaping, until the marks of His workmanship are unmistakable. That is how it should be.

When a house has been occupied by someone for a long while, it begins to reveal His personality, His tastes, His pleasures and fulfillments, and we see this often when we go into homes. Just so, the fruits of the Spirit begin to appear where He is dwelling, as old features of the believer give way, step by step, to the likeness of Christ. The man is changed from glory to glory when the Lord the Spirit is at work.

MARCH 29

"These are such as in an honest and good heart, having heard the word, hold it fast and bring forth fruit with patience." Luke 8:15

The question has been raised, how do you reconcile God's requirements of "an honest and good heart" with the statement that "the heart is deceitful above all things"? But the point in the parable of the sower is not that the man who receives the Word is a perfectly honest man in God's eyes, but that he is honest toward God. Whatever is in his heart, he is prepared to come to God frankly and openly with it. It is possible for a man with a deceitful nature to turn honestly to God.

This is what God seeks in men, and something of this meaning is contained in the Lord's promise to "show Himself strong in the behalf of them whose heart is perfect toward Him." The basic condition of a sinner's salvation is not belief, but just this honesty of heart toward God. God requires nothing of him but that he come in that attitude. Into that spot of straightforwardness that lies in the midst of much deceit, the good seed falls and brings forth fruit.

MARCH 30

"Thy testimonies are wonderful; therefore doth my soul keep them." Psalm 119:129

There is something about the Lord Jesus which is altogether more than His work. He is himself a testimony to the nature of God. He is the only One who could say, "I delight to do thy will, O my God." That is why God has entrusted the outworking of the eternal purpose to Him.

How, then, do we bear testimony? By putting the Lord Jesus in the central and supreme place. Of course He will be supreme in the kingdom of God that is to come, but we must not wait for everything to happen then. The faithful witness to God's kingdom is careful to give Christ that place of supremacy here and now.

MARCH 31

"We who died to sin, how shall we any longer live therein?" Romans 6:2

Let us be careful not to separate into two the death of the Lord Jesus as our substitute and our death with Him. Those who find pleasure in intellectual distinctions are apt to confuse us by doing so, but in spiritual life these two are one. His substitutionary death for our sins and our death with Him to sin and self should be distinguished but never separated. Paul clearly affirms here in Romans that those who believe in the death of the Lord Jesus as their Savior have already died to sin.

The penalty for my sin is death. The Lord Jesus suffered this death for me; therefore, I have died in Him. There can be no salvation otherwise. To say that He died for me is to say that I have already suffered sin's penalty and died in him. Everyone who lays hold of this reality will experience its power of deliverance from sin and self in his daily living.

APRIL 1

"Tattlers also and busybodies, speaking things which they ought not." 1 Timothy 5:13

Several things about this matter of speech deserve our attention. In the first place, we should consider the kind of talk we enjoy listening to. In this way we can get to know ourselves. Do people come to us because they find that they can pour all the latest gossip into our ears? The sort of talk we relish indicates the kind of people we are. In the second place, we should observe what tales we most readily credit. We are mostly more gullible in one direction than in others, and the direction of our gullibility betrays our innate weakness. Are we quick to believe the slanders of talebearers? People naturally bring supply to demand. Do we show them that it is unwelcome?

But it is those who need our help who really test us. Do people find in us those to whom they can confide their real heart problems and be met with understanding and wise counsel? Are we sensitive enough, and close enough to God, for that?

APRIL 2

"His heart is fixed, trusting in Jehovah. His heart is established." Psalm 112:7, 8

From start to finish the Christian experience is a journey of faith. Through it we come into possession of a new life, and through it we walk by that new life. We live by faith and not by joy. Joy is wonderful, but it feeds our sensations and lures us into seeking the things above only at times of excitement. Should our blissful feelings cease, our interest wanes. That is not the walk of faith.

Our feelings are always changing. He is the same God everyday, be it cloudy or sunny. Are we trusting in the up-and-down existence of our feelings, or is our faith anchored in the Unchanging One?

"That Christ may dwell in your hearts through faith."
Ephesians 3:17

The life of the Christian resembles the situation in God's tabernacle of old. There the outer precinct was a scene of bustling activity, the inner sanctuary a place of stillness. A great number of Levites were needed to prepare the many offerings and must have filled the court to overflowing from morning till night; but in the Most Holy Place there was not a man to be found. The screen of the outer court must frequently have parted to let people in; but the veil before the Holiest hung quite still, undisturbed by the entry of anyone. Outside, the din and movement spoke of busy ritual service; inside there remained a quiet place apart.

Such is the Christian life. Without, you may be in constant touch with people, yet within be undisturbed. The outward busyness need provoke no ripples in the spirit. And since you live before God in constant communion with Him inwardly, you have what is needed for the outward occupation of serving men who seek and need Him.

APRIL 4

"Where then is the glorying? It is excluded."
Romans 3:27

We shall best understand the call of Abraham if we see it in its proper setting. The nations all around had not only forgotten God, but were idolaters. The whole world worshiped false gods, and Abraham's family was no exception. In this Abraham was very different from Abel, Enoch, and Noah, who seem to have been men of backbone, strikingly different from all those around them. They stood out against the stream and refused to be dragged along by it. Not so Abraham. He was indistinguishable from those around him. Were they idolaters? So was he.

God, however, chose him. It was clearly not in Abraham's moral character that we must seek the reason for this choice, but in God Himself. If Abraham had not been just the same as all the rest, then in looking back he might have prided himself on his difference. But he was one of them. As with you and me, the difference lay in God and not in the man. So I ask you: Who should receive the glory?

❧

APRIL 5

"And what hast thou that thou didst not receive? but if thou didst receive it, why dost thou glory . . .?" 1
Corinthians 4:7

When the Lord Jesus entered Jerusalem riding on a colt, the crowds shouted in acclamation. Let us suppose for a moment that the colt, upon hearing the cry of hosanna and seeing the branches on the road, should turn to the Lord and ask, "Is this cry for You or for me?" or should turn to the ass, its mother, and say, "After all, I was the one chosen; so I am nobler than you." It would be evident that the colt did not recognize the One who rode upon it.

Many of us who are God's servants are just as foolish. God's sovereign choice of whom He may use reflects no credit on us at all. It is He whom we uplift who is to be praised. The shouts of hosanna are never for us, nor are the palm branches, though we should discover them beneath our feet. And as for us fools who would say, "I am better than you"—one day we shall wake up to the truth and be utterly ashamed of ourselves.

APRIL 6

"And the world passeth away, and the lust thereof: but
he that doeth the will of God abideth for ever."
1 John 2:17

Our deliverance from the world begins, not with our giving up this or that but with our seeing, as with God's eyes, that it is a world under sentence of death. It has no future. Suppose the government decides to close a certain bank. Will you hasten to deposit into it a large sum of money in order to save the bank from collapse? No, not a cent more do you pay into it, once you hear that it offers no prospects. And we may justly say of the world that it is under a decree of closure.

Babylon, an impressive figure of world power, fell when her champions made war with the Lamb, and when by His death and resurrection He who is Lord of lords and King of kings overcame them (Revelation 17:14). There is no future for her. We still go on living in the world and using the things of the world, but we can build no future with them, for everything belonging to this world is under sentence of destruction.

APRIL 7

"And he said unto him, Verily I say unto thee, Today shalt thou be with me in Paradise." Luke 23:43

Suppose that this malefactor who was crucified with Christ had lived on after he had believed in the Lord. Suppose he had come down from the cross and lived for several decades more. Let us further suppose that during those years his work had been ten times more than that of Paul, that his love had grown ten times more than John's, and that he had brought ten times more people to Christ than Peter did.

Would it have made any difference if he had gone to heaven then, rather than on the day on which he was crucified? Would he have been any worthier of his place there after all those years?

All who have tasted the grace of God know that he would not have been one whit worthier than when he entered Paradise on that first day. Qualification for heaven is founded on Christ's "It is finished." No one can add anything to His work of redemption.

APRIL 8

"There is nothing among my treasures that I have not showed them." Isaiah 39:4

Hezekiah was the prosperous king of a historic little country. The king of Babylon was the ruler of a growing powerful one. His congratulations to Hezekiah on the occasion of the latter's miraculous recovery from illness seemed thus genuinely flattering. Hezekiah felt his stature enhanced by them: he was mixing with the great ones. Because his vanity had been thus boosted, he betrayed himself into a foolish exposure of all his treasures.

Like him, we are all too ready to be glad when attention is paid to us, whether by men or by God. If one soul is saved or healed when we are involved, or if people are helped by something we have said, then we are flattered and begin to expose the sacred treasures of God by recounting them to others. But God, through His prophet, soon made it clear to Hezekiah that such behavior leads only to loss. Let us seek grace, rather, to be silent before Him.

APRIL 9

"One that ruleth over men righteously, that ruleth in the fear of God . . ." 2 Samuel 23:3

David is so often called in Scripture "King David" because he was a true king in spirit as well as in title. He was a king at heart. When a giant threatened Israel, Saul trembled and so did all the people. Only David was unafraid. There is no fear in the heart of a king.

Ah, but David feared God. Saul became envious and persecuted him, driving him into exile. Then, on at least two occasions, David found Saul at his mercy and had the opportunity of killing him. Nevertheless, without a command from God he would not lift a finger against his oppressor. Whoever cannot control his own spirit is no king. A true king is a king under all circumstances; he reigns everywhere.

APRIL 10

"The seven golden lampstands [margin] are seven
churches." Revelation 1:20

In Revelation 2 and 3, we are shown the Son
of Man moving among the lampstands and
affirming the individual responsibility of each
to Himself. Our eyes, following His, readily de-
tect the many failures in the churches; but has
it occurred to us that John nowhere distinguishes between the churches that are right and the
churches that are wrong? For all their faultiness,
he writes of them as the Lord himself still sees
them: namely, as "seven golden lampstands,"
seven candlesticks all of gold.

What God is doing through men is eternal—
not just something for ten or twenty years. What
God has in view He will never abandon, for the
very good reason that He Himself never changes.
A person who cannot afford to wear true pearls
buys paste beads and thinks of them as imitation
pearls. But to the one who has real pearls there
is no such thing as imitation pearls. To her there
are not real pearls and false pearls; there are only
pearls.

APRIL 11

*"And she called his name Moses, and said, Because I
drew him out of the water." Exodus 2:10*

Had Moses not been drawn out of the water,
Israel might have remained in bondage.
It was his exodus from death in the Nile which
made possible Israel's exodus from Egypt. Triumphant over Egypt because never in its bondage, he became God's instrument for delivering
his people from Egypt's king.

In this, of course, he is a wonderful figure
of Christ our Redeemer, who voluntarily identi-
fied Himself with us to the extent of becoming
one of us, and yet never knew bondage to Satan
or the world. By His exodus from death he has
made possible our exodus from bondage. And
it is He who leads us on in our pilgrim way to
God's prepared inheritance.

APRIL 12

"The anointing which ye received of him abideth in you . . . his anointing teacheth you concerning all things."
1 John 2:27

The anointing of the Spirit is God's gift to every babe in Christ. When we received Christ as Head, we received the anointing—indeed the absence of it would be serious evidence that we were not yet united to Him.

John shows us this anointing as an inward thing, conveying even to those babes in Christ the teaching of the Scriptures "concerning all things." Herein lies the simplicity of the life of God's children. There is no need for so much questioning. Disobedience to the anointing will very soon give us a bad time with the Lord, whereas the mind of the Spirit is life and peace. It is not a question of feeling or comparison, but of an inquiry Godward: "Does the Spirit witness life? Does He assure me of the Father's good pleasure in this step?" That is the only safe test.

"Ye are in our hearts to die together and live together."
2 Corinthians 7:3

Paul was one whose whole being could be involved in the words he wrote. In a moral crisis such as the one he had to deal with at Corinth he could not just dash off a letter. What he wrote was wrung out of his heart through pain and tears. He was not like one who speaks with an unknown tongue, with words coming in and going out without so much as touching the thoughts of his heart.

There will always be a human element in our work for God, whether it be counseling or the preaching of the Word. Unless the counsel we give or the word we preach is capable of causing us real joy or real anguish of heart, we might as well be dictating machines, first recording every word faithfully and then playing it back verbatim. No, God delights to use ordinary, sensitive men and women as His messengers.

APRIL 14

"Look ye out therefore, brethren, from among you seven men of good report, full of the Spirit and of wisdom, whom we may appoint over this business." Acts 6:3

The occasion was a contingency which led the Church to institute relief for the poorer saints. That urgent institution of social service was clearly blessed of God, but it was of a temporary nature. Do you exclaim, "How good if it had continued"? Only one who does not know God would say that. Had those relief measures been prolonged indefinitely, they would certainly have veered in the direction of selfish interests, once the spiritual influence at work at their inception was removed. It would have been inevitable.

When material things are under spiritual control, they fulfill their subordinate role. Released from that restraint, they quickly gravitate toward worldly standards and goals. The Church of God, however, is different. She never ceases to be dependent on the life of God for her maintenance.

APRIL 15

*"And for their sakes I sanctify myself, that they them-
selves also may be sanctified in truth." John 17:19*

As the sinless Son of God, Jesus enjoyed a
freedom far exceeding any we have on earth.
There is much that we may not do or say because
we are so full of defects and defilement, but that
was never true of Him. And yet, notwithstanding
his faultlessness, he deliberately refrained from
doing many things which, for him, would have
been quite legitimate, from speaking many words
which He might lawfuly have spoken, and from
taking many attitudes which He could justifi-
ably have taken. These were some of the ways in
which He "sanctified" Himself, refraining from
much that was lawful for His disciples' sake.

What it means is that when holiness was in
view, the Lord Jesus thought not merely of His
own holiness, but of ours. For our sakes He accepted limitations. The opposite of holiness is
not sin but commonness. Commonness means:
I do what is common practice to everyone. Holiness means: others may do something, but, in
this instance at least, I may not. To sanctify ourselves is to accept restraint from God upon our

spirits. As with the Lord Jesus, this may often be for the sake of others.

❧

APRIL 16

"He set the bounds of the peoples according to the number of the children of Israel." Deuteronomy 32:8

In the centuries when China was strong, there was no opportunity for the progress of the gospel. Then came a period of a hundred years when she was at her weakest. God in wisdom ordained this for the building of His Church. He was holding a door open for Chinese to find Christ. In relation to earthly nations and events, the supreme question to ask ourselves is always, how is the Church of God affected? This should be the direction of all our prayers with regard to world governments—not for or against one side or another, in politics or war, but for the will of God.

If all history is in relation to the Lord's testimony, then we must know how to pray. It must be possible for British and German, Chinese and Japanese Christians to kneel together and pray together, and all say Amen. Our one appeal to God must be for a march of events that is of advantage to the testimony of His Son.

APRIL 17

"The disciples were called Christians first in Antioch."
Acts 11:26

The Bible uses the name Christian, meaning "Christ-man" or "Christ's one," but never does it say "Jesus-man." Jesus is a personal name, whereas Christ is a name that is inclusive as well as personal. The Christian is a part of Christ, a member of the Body of which He is Head (1 Corinthians 12:12). We rejoice to call ourselves Christians.

The name Jesus applies essentially to the Son of Man in His experience on earth. While Jesus lived here on earth, He revealed Himself as unique among all men in virtue and beauty. None could approach Him and none could be united with Him as Son of Man. But the meaning of the name Jesus is also "savior." He comes down to us to save us from our sins, and while we can never unite with Him in His saviorhood, by death and resurrection He has lifted us up to union with Himself as the exalted Christ on the throne.

APRIL 18

"But the priests the Levites . . . shall come near to me to minister unto me." Ezekiel 44:15

O ne condition basic to all that can truly be called ministry to the Lord is that we draw near to Him. He desires our worship; yet how hard we find it to drag ourselves into His presence! We shrink from the solitude, and even when we do detach ourselves physically from outside things, we find our thoughts wandering back to them.

Many of us can enjoy working among people in the outer court, but how many of us give time to draw near to God in the Holy Place? To come into His presence and wait upon Him demands all the determination we possess, and even means that we may have to be violent with ourselves. But let me be very frank with you: it is impossible to stand afar off and yet minister to Him. You cannot serve God from a distance. In the outer court, quite rightly, you approach people; in the Holy Place you approach the Lord. Come nearer. It is your privilege.

APRIL 19

"Christ being raised from the dead dieth no more; death no more bath dominion over him." Romans 6:9

The resurrection of the Lord Jesus is different from the resurrection of other people mentioned in the Bible. For example, in calling Lazarus out of the grave Jesus merely returned him to the life-situation he had just left. He was even still bound with grave-clothes, and until loosened from them could not walk freely.

When Peter and John ran to the tomb of Jesus and entered in, they saw the wound grave-clothes lying empty with no body inside. Unlike Lazarus, the Lord Jesus had passed out through them unbound. Nothing, absolutely nothing, could restrict Him any more. Before His resurrection, He too was subject to human limitations; after it, He knew no restriction at all. Death could not hold Him, and now nothing would.

APRIL 20

"Jesus Christ is the same yesterday and today, yea and forever." Hebrews 13:8

Spiritual reality has this outstanding characteristic, that it bears no mark of time. The time-factor vanishes the instant you touch that reality. Take, for example, prophecy. From the human point of view there is such a thing as prophecy, but from the divine point of view no such thing exists.

Our Lord says that He is the First and the Last, the Alpha and Omega; but remember, He is both together, both at once. It is not true that at one time He is First and at another time He is Last; He is the First and Last simultaneously. Nor is it that having for a while been Alpha, He later on becomes Omega; He is Alpha and Omega from eternity to eternity. Of course in the sight of men He is not Omega until He is so manifested, but in the sight of God He is Omega now. With me the "I" of yesterday differs from the "I" of today, and the "I" of tomorrow differs still further; but Jesus Christ is the eternal "I AM."

APRIL 21

"The joy of Jehovah is your strength." Nehemiah 8:10

The worst kind of life to live is the life of reactions, in which we are all the time affected by persons or circumstances. When we speak and somebody responds warmly to our words, we are full of joy; but we are the very opposite when our message is not well received. Being thus easily affected will inevitably produce an up-and-down experience. Don't mistake me—it is natural to feel things deeply, but he who is governed by such feelings will always be lacking in divine strength.

It is when we lose our joy that our strength seeps away. The joy of the Lord Jesus when He was here on earth never rested on the seeming success of His mission. It was not in fact attributable to anything outward, but only to His steadfast pursuit of the will of the Father—"the joy that was set before Him." Thank God that we do not have to try to copy Jesus, but only to keep our eyes on His goal. His joy is ours by the Holy Spirit.

APRIL 22

"These things have I spoken unto you, that my joy may be in you, and that your joy may be made full."
John 15:11

From Watchman Nee's last letter, dated April 22, 1972, in his sixty-ninth year, after twenty years in confinement and shortly before his death:

"You know my physical condition. It is a chronic illness—it is always with me. When it strikes, it causes pain. Even if it should be dormant, it is nonetheless there. The difference is whether it strikes or not. Recovery is out of the question. In summer the sun can add some color to my skin, but it cannot cure my illness. But I maintain the joy in me.

Please don't be anxious. I hope you will also take good care of yourself, and be filled with joy! All the best to you."

APRIL 23

"Who were born not . . . of the will of the flesh, nor of the will of man, but of God." John 1:13

The recurring phrase "after its kind" in Genesis 1 represents a law of reproduction that governs the whole realm of biological nature. It does not, however, govern the realm of the Spirit. For generation after generation, human parents can beget children after their kind, but one thing is certain: Christians cannot beget Christians! Not even when both parents are Christians will the children born to them automatically be Christians, no, not even in the first generation.

That which is born of the flesh is flesh, and that which is born of the Spirit is spirit. It will take a fresh act of God every time to produce someone who is truly a child of His.

❧

APRIL 24

"Honor thy father and mother (which is the first commandment with promise)." Ephesians 6:2

When I was a young man at college, God showed me I was to go on my vacation to an island which was infested with pirates, to preach the gospel. I visited the island and found the people willing, and after much difficulty I rented a house there. All this time my parents had said nothing and then, five days before I was to go, they suddenly stepped in and forbade it! What was I to do? The will of God was burning in my heart, but my parents, God-fearing folk, said "No." I was still a student. I sought light from God and felt it right to submit to my parents, though deeply wounded.

In God's time the way to that island was opened, and His will that souls should be won there came wonderfully to pass. But this experience had taught me an important lesson. If a thing is written in the Word of God, we dare not cast it aside—we have to submit.

❧

APRIL 25

*"The hearing ear, and the seeing eye, Jehovah hath
made even both of them." Proverbs 20:12*

Alas, very few Christians are good listeners!
We shall have to take ourselves rigorously
in hand if we are to acquire hearing ears. Our
ears must be trained to listen. It is possible to
pay scant attention to what people say to us, because we are so impressed with the importance
of what we wish to communicate to them. We
are just waiting for an opportunity to break in
and take up the role of speaker again, assuming,
naturally, that they will meekly accept the role of
good listeners!

Let us not consider this a trifling matter.
If we do not learn to listen, and listen under-
standingly, although we may become prominent
preachers or Bible expositors, we shall be useless
at helping people to deal with their practical difficulties. There are far more times when we need
to learn to use our ears than to open our mouths.

APRIL 26

"And having gifts differing according to the grace that was given to us . . . let us give ourselves to our ministry." Romans 12:6, 7

The calling of God is a distinctive calling. Moreover, its object is always precise, never merely haphazard or undefined. By this I mean that when God commits to you or to me a ministry He does so, not merely to occupy us in his service, but always to accomplish through each of us something definite toward the attaining of His goal. It is of course true that there is a general commission to His Church to "make disciples of all the nations"; but to any one of us, God's charge represents, and must always represent, a personal trust.

It follows from this that since God does not call each of His servants to precisely identical tasks, neither does He use precisely identical means for their preparation. As the Lord of all operations, God retains the right to use particular forms of discipline or training and often, too, the added test of suffering, as means to His end. God understands clearly what He is doing with you.

APRIL 27

"Now unto him that is able to do exceedingly abundantly above all that we ask or think, according to the power that worketh in us . . ." Ephesians 3:20

God's glory for endless ages is to be "in the church and in Christ Jesus" (verse 21). But God's glory now, in the exercise of that exceedingly abundant power of His, is to be dependent on the Church, for here we see it measured according to the power that now works in us.

His people are thus the gateway of the power of God. What God wants to do here in time is narrowed down to limits set by their cooperation. Must we not therefore revive our ministry of prayer? The purpose of God here in Shanghai and throughout China—indeed worldwide—depends on the Church's prayer ministry today. "Ask," said Jesus, "and ye shall receive." If we fail in this simple task, what use are we to God at all?

APRIL 28

"Wherefore is it that thou dost ask after my name? And he blessed him there." Genesis 32:29

After his struggle at Jabbok Jacob wanted to know who "touched him," but he was not told. Jacob did not know who the Wrestler was when he came, and he knew no more when he went. Jacob just knew that his own name had been changed—and that he limped! This is the only time in Scripture when God declined to reveal His name to a servant of His.

Those touched by God do not know what has happened. That is why the touch is so difficult to define, for God does not want us to wait for an experience. If we do, we shall not get it. God wants our eye fixed on Him, not on experiences. Jacob only knew that somehow God had met him, and that now he was crippled. The limp is the evidence. When God does His work in us in His own way, the result will be evident in us, and there will be no need to talk about it.

✒

APRIL 29

"For to me to live is Christ." Philippians 1:21

On the evening of April 29, 1920, I was alone in my room, struggling to decide whether or not to believe in the Lord. At first I was reluctant, but as I tried to pray I saw the magnitude of my sins and the reality and efficacy of Jesus as the Savior. As I visualized His hands stretched out on the cross, they seemed to be welcoming me and He was saying, "I am waiting here to receive you." Realizing the effectiveness of His blood in cleansing my sins and being overwhelmed by such love, I accepted Him there.

Previously I had laughed at people who had accepted Jesus, but that evening the experience became real for me and I wept and confessed my sins, seeking the Lord's forgiveness. As I made my first prayer, I knew peace and joy such as I had never known before. Light seemed to flood the room and I said to him, "O Lord, You have indeed been gracious to me!"

APRIL 30

"I say unto you, this man went down to his house justi-fied." Luke 18:14

At most the publican could only plead for forgiveness. God heard his prayer, but gave him much more than he had asked for, since Jesus said that he returned home "justified." Do you see how far this exceeded the sinner's expectations? He asked for mercy; he could never think of justification. But God said that he was justified. This means that it was as if he had never sinned. Not only was he no longer sinful: now he was actually righteous.

The salvation which God accomplishes is not according to our limited measure, but to his infinite grace. Man has his small ideas of how God will act on his behalf, but God likes to hear his cry and answer his prayers. But what He brings to pass accords with His own disposition as the lavish dispenser of unmerited favor. Let us praise Him!

MAY 1

"Having put off from himself [margin] the principali-
ties and the powers, he made a show of them openly."
Colossians 2:15

How did the Lord Jesus put Satan to shame? By shaking off from Himself the powers of evil as He rose from the dead. Resurrection implies a realm beyond the touch of death. Men die, animals and plants die; all living things are subject to death. There is no exception, for death has spread like a net over this entire world. It has entered into every living thing. But here is a Man who came out of death, for death could not retain Him.

The life we receive at the time of new birth is this resurrection life. This life has no relationship whatever to Satan. Always remember that his attacks on us can never exceed his attacks on our Lord at the cross. There all his efforts were exerted and all proved of no avail. He was overcome, and from that day he is the defeated foe. We give thanks to God because He has given us the victory in Christ.

MAY 2

"He spake unadvisedly with his lips." Psalm 106:33

After more than thirty years of proving God in the wilderness, the people of Israel were still rebellious, and quick to blame Moses and Aaron for the lack of water. For His part God was ready to meet their needs, and commanded His servant to take His rod and speak to the rock that it might give water. Moses took the rod, but he was so provoked by the people's unjust accusations that he spoke to them in anger and then struck the rock twice. He erred; yet the water flowed freely from the rock.

Because of this, God reprimanded His servant. It was as though he remonstrated, "I saw that My people were thirsty and was willing to provide water for them, so why did you scold them?" Clearly Moses had given the people the wrong impression of God as fierce and unmerciful. Let us be warned by this never to draw God into human failure by giving to others the impression that the faulty attitudes we display are His.

MAY 3

"I coveted no man's silver, or gold, or apparel." Acts
20:33

Paul made no contract with the church in Ephesus, or with any other church, that he should receive a certain remuneration for a certain period of service. That God's servants should look to human sources for the supply of their needs has no precedent in Scripture. We do read there of a Balaam who sought to make merchandise of his gift of prophecy, but he is denounced in no uncertain terms. We read also of a Gehazi who sought to make gain of the grace of God, but he was stricken with leprosy for his sin.

No servant of God should look to any human agency for the meeting of his temporal needs. If they can be met by the labor of his own hands, well and good; otherwise he should be directly dependent on God alone for their supply.

MAY 4

"Knowing this first, that no prophecy of scripture is of private interpretation." 2 Peter 1:20

The word "private" points not to the inter-preter but to the words being interpreted. It means that prophetic Scripture is not to be explained by its own context alone. For example, Matthew 24 should be read in the light of other Scriptures which bear on it. For no prophecy is self-interpreting; a given passage will be understood with the help of many other passages. To attempt otherwise is to fall into "private interpretation."

Truly God's Word is one. He has set it in writing in the Bible; hence we have no need to speak independently, but can check our words by what has already been spoken by God. No doubt God the Holy Spirit gives us new insights and discoveries of his will, but our safeguard is that all can be founded on what God has already spoken. We should never move away from that.

MAY 5

"Look therefore carefully how ye walk, not as unwise, but as wise, redeeming the time, because the days are evil." Ephesians 5:15, 16

With the parable of the ten virgins, the contrast between the wise and the foolish was over the matter of readiness. Here a similar contrast is made, for the wise are described as those who buy up the opportunity. The unwise are like the child who imagines that by procrastination he may perhaps avoid the need for obedience. If in fact this policy of doing nothing is successful, then in a sense he will have been wise.

If, however, the command is insisted upon and must ultimately be obeyed, then it is sheer folly to delay. The passage goes on to say that to avoid foolishness we must get clear about God's will. If our God is an unchanging God with an unalterable purpose of good, then it is our wisdom to give Him prompt obedience without wasting unnecessary time.

MAY 6

"And he prayed again; and the heaven gave rain, and the earth brought forth her fruit." James 5:18

The Lord had explicitly told Elijah to seek out King Ahab because he was about to send rain on the earth. He did not, however, send this rain until Elijah had prayed. God does not always carry out His will alone; He waits for us to cooperate with Him by prayer. It is true that Elijah needed first to know it was God's will and that his time to act had at last come; but knowing this did not excuse him from that earnest prayer which released the rain.

It is a mistake to think that man initiates anything by prayer. The Bible shows us that it is God who first desires to do certain things, and make His wishes known. Our part is to learn what is His will and then to ask Him to perform it. This can truly be called prayer, and it is what God wants from us.

≈

MAY 7

"Brethren, even if a man be overtaken in any trespass, ye who are spiritual, restore such a one in a spirit of meekness." Galatians 6:1

Discipline is always a remedial measure, and has as its object the recovery of the sinning brother. Even in the most extreme case of church discipline, the end in view is "that the spirit may be saved in the day of the Lord Jesus." Where God's children are concerned, there is mercy in all His judgment; and when we judge any of His children on His behalf, whether we do so as the whole church or as individual members, we should be full of mercy. Even though our outward attitude may have to be one of discipline, our inner attitude should be one of love.

The Lord states very clearly what our object should be in the case of any offense. It is not the winning of our case but the gaining of our brother. Even one in spiritual advance of others dare not take a "better-than-thou" position. We must first locate in ourselves the sin that is manifest in our brother, and not till we have judged that in ourselves dare we judge it in him.

MAY 8

"Jesus I know, and Paul I know; but who are ye?"
Acts 19:15

We talk sometimes about our desire to maintain, like John, the testimony of Jesus on earth. Let us remember that this testimony is based not on what we can say about this or that, but on what Satan can say about us. God has put us in this world, and often He locates us in some specially difficult places, where we are tempted to feel that worldlings have a much easier time than do Christians.

The question is: Of what account are we in the realm of principalities and powers? Evil spirits can see right through the witness of man. They can tell when it is compromised by half-heartedness or insincerity. Because they believe, they know when to tremble. And let me say this: since our most important task is their overthrow, it is better always that we should have the witness of evil powers than the praise of men.

≈

MAY 9

"And Samuel grew, and Jehovah was with him, and
did let none of his words fall to the ground."
1 Samuel 3:19

Samuel was not only a child given in answer to
his mother's prayer; he was one who very early learned to pray himself. He stands as a complete contrast to the priest Eli, who was not only
old in years but dull as to spiritual things, no
longer having faculties tuned to communicate
with God. The very first time God called him,
Samuel was alert to hear; and although he did
not at once recognize that the voice was God's,
he was quick to learn and to obey.

This led on to a prayer-life worthy of comparison with that of Moses. Samuel became a living link between the old and the new, between
the sad declension of Israel under the judges
and the glorious reign of David. If prayer could
bridge such a gap then, it can do such things
today.

❧

MAY 10

"This mystery is great: but I speak in regard of Christ and of the church." Ephesians 5:32

God's purpose in creating the Church is that she may be the help meet for Christ. He had said, "Let us make man in our image . . . and let them have dominion" (Genesis 1:26). The same pattern is used in the following verse: "In the image of God created He him; male and female created He them." So God created one man, but we might also say that in that act He created two persons. Eve was in Adam at his creation.

However, it was by being taken from Adam that Eve was formed. Now in a different, but parallel sense, the Church is formed from Christ, and only that which originates with Christ can be the Church. The Church is the Christ in you, and the Christ in all the Christians around the world throughout all the centuries, put together in one. Without Christ, she has no existence, no life, and no future. But dare we not also say that without her—without you and me—He lacks the help meet for Him?

MAY 11

"Philip answered him, 'Two hundred shillings' worth of bread is not sufficient for them.'" John 6:7

Have you noticed that the Gospels record two separate miracles in which Christ feeds a great company of people? Why two, when they were almost identical in nature and in the way they were performed? Is it perhaps because of our slowness to learn even urgent lessons?

So many of us, instead of looking to the Lord to bless the bread, are looking down at the five loaves in our hands. They are so pitifully few, and so pitifully small. We gaze at them, and we calculate, and we keep on wondering how they can ever meet the need. And the more we calculate and the more we wonder, the more laborious our attempts become and the more we are exhausted by the strain. I am comforted when I recall what a Chinese brother once said to me. It was this: "When God wants to perform a small miracle, He places us in difficult circumstances; when He wants to perform a mighty miracle, the circumstances in which He places us are impossible."

MAY 12

"Now I know that thou fearest God." Genesis 22:12

One who has become pliable in God's hand instantly responds to any fresh desire of his. Just at the point when Abraham placed Isaac on the altar and raised the knife to slay him, God called to him to stay his hand and showed him a ram which he should offer instead of his son. This might well have posed a new problem for Abraham. How could he ever discern God's will if at one moment He told him to do one thing and the next moment the very reverse?

If we attach our own thoughts to the will of God, then of course when He changes his commands our thoughts will remain fixed. We shall then wonder how possibly to be consistent! For Abraham, however, all was perfectly simple and straightforward. His instant obedience was not to reason but to trust God in all circumstances. This left no room for perplexity. In this he gives us a beautiful picture of a man who has been saved from himself, a man who truly fears God.

MAY 13

"Thy name is as ointment poured forth; therefore do the
virgins love thee." Song of Songs 1:3

The Lord Jesus is Himself the Anointed One,
the Christ. Like sweet and fragrant anointing oil, the Holy Spirit makes known to both
God and men the beauties of His holy life. The
fact, however, that the sweet ointment of His
precious name is spoken of as being poured forth
makes us think immediately of our Lord's death.

At His Table we do more than remember that death: we proclaim it (1 Corinthians
11:26). Our remembrance includes that death,
but goes beyond it to the Lord Himself, for he
said, "Do this in remembrance of Me." Most of
us will agree that nothing is more stimulating
to memory than some specific scent—the smell
of a hay field perhaps—associated with a moving experience of the past. So it is that we think
gratefully not only of what He has done, but
of His Person. The virgins do not merely love
mercies and benefits; they love the Person whose
name has become so sweet to them.

MAY 14

"Then he shall minister in the name of Jehovah his God, as all his brethren the Levites do, which stand there before Jehovah." Deuteronomy 18:7

Those who minister to God must not only draw near to Him; they must stand before him. It seems to me that nowadays we always want to be moving about; we cannot stand still. There are so many things claiming our attention that we are perpetually on the go. A spiritual person, however, must know how to stand still. He stands before God until God makes His will known.

Brethren, do you not think that any servant should await his master's orders before seeking to serve him? I wish to address myself especially to my fellow-workers. There are only two types of sin before God in this matter of service. One is the sin of refusing to obey His commands. The other is the sin of going ahead when the Lord has not issued orders. The one is rebellion: the other is presumption. It is standing before the Lord that delivers us from this second sin of doing what He has not commanded. It is our privilege to await His pleasure.

MAY 15

"The spirit indeed is willing, but the flesh is weak."
Matthew 26:41

The disciples are in Gethsemane. In every sense, therefore, this is a pre-Pentecost experience. It reminds us that the Christian cannot live by his own willpower. The greatest willpower can only bring to the point of willingness—no further. To be willing cannot give strength to the weak flesh. Something much more than that is needed.

Willpower is like a car without gas. It has to be pushed or towed. Left to itself, it grinds to a halt. To trust to the human will for spiritual ends is therefore to encounter defeat. Spiritual power does not come from the human will, but from the new life in Christ. This life provides another, deeper power beyond our volition, and by that Power we find ourselves gloriously carried along in the Lord's victory.

MAY 16

"Who his own self bare our sins in his body upon the tree." 1 Peter 2:24

Man sins through his body and in that body enjoys the temporary pleasure of sin. The body must accordingly bear the judgment due to sin. This partly explains the physical sufferings of our Savior. His sufferings in His body are clearly foretold in the messianic writings. His hands, His feet, His brow, His side, His heart were all pierced at Calvary; pierced not only by sinful men, but pierced for sinful humanity.

The hands must be nailed, for the hands love to sin. The mouth must become parched, for it is so often an instrument of sin. The feet must be transfixed, for they lead into sin. The brow must be pierced by a thorny crown, for it too loves to sin. All that the human body needed to suffer was executed upon His holy body. It was within His power to avoid these sufferings, yet He willingly offered His body to endure immeasurable pains for us, only dismissing His Spirit when He was sure that all had been accomplished.

MAY 17

"And the scripture, foreseeing that God would justify the Gentiles by faith, preached the gospel beforehand unto Abraham." Galatians 3:8

Paul reminds us that grace does not begin with the New Testament. What God gave to Abraham was not the law, but the promise of the gospel. According to Galatians, today's gospel is based upon the gospel spoken to Abraham; our blessing is founded upon the blessing of Abraham; the promise we have today is traced back to God's promise to Abraham; and even the Christ we receive is the seed of Abraham. Paul demonstrates to us that the Old Testament and the New form a straight line.

To put it differently: God has not at one time given us grace and at another time law; neither has He bestowed the promise and then demanded work for a while. The grace we receive today is not something new, but is the same grace which Abraham received. Thus the promise at first, the law in between, and the finished work of Christ afterwards all fall into one straight line.

MAY 18

"In Christ Jesus I begat you through the gospel."
1 Corinthians 4:15

Abraham, so we are told, is the father of all them who believe. This is an interesting expression, for it shows us that all true spirituality is based on birth and not on preaching. Men are not changed by listening to doctrine or by following a course of instructive teaching. They are changed by birth.

First God chose one man who believed, and from him were born the many. When an unbeliever meets a man who has been saved by believing, he becomes aware that this man has something he does not possess. That something is not just information; it is life. He has been born again. Those who have this seed of life in them should, like Abraham, be giving birth to others. Paul's words here about his sons in the faith show that he was not merely their preacher or counselor, but their spiritual father.

MAY 19

"In lowliness of mind each counting other better than himself." Philippians 2:3

An elderly Christian who had served the Lord for many decades was once asked, "What is the most difficult to achieve of all Christian virtues?" "Lowliness of mind," was the answer. "To count the other better than myself is the problem." "Then what do you do?" "There is only one thing to do. When I consider myself, I look at my 'old man' as Paul calls it; but when I consider another, I look at his 'new man'—the new creation he is in Christ."

How readily we criticize others! Our expectations of them are even higher than the Lord's, who demands little and forgives much. What we see are their obvious failures, but what the Lord sees are their hidden victories. My brother's failures lie on the surface, but the victories he has won in secret may exceed any I have experienced myself or ever dreamed of.

ᕊᎯᎩ 20

"Lest by any means, as the serpent beguiled Eve in his craftiness, your thoughts should be corrupted from the simplicity and the purity that is toward Christ."
2 Corinthians 11:3

Before a man can receive a new heart from God, he needs to have a change of mind. This is what happens at conversion. Even after this, however, the believer's mind is not exempt from the assaults of Satan. The same apostle who affirmed that the god of this world had blinded the minds of unbelievers was also concerned lest Satan should deceive and corrupt the thoughts of those who had experienced this change of mind.

In deceiving Eve by his craftiness, Satan first put doubting thoughts into her mind. At that time her heart was sinless. Yet she allowed her thoughts to be distorted, so forfeiting her reason and spoiling her relationship with God. Let us be careful of boasting about the sincerity of our hearts while being careless concerning our thought-life. Transformation depends on the renewing of the mind.

MAY 21

"I dwell in the high and holy place, with him also that is of a contrite and humble spirit." Isaiah 57:15

As God's people we may think, erroneously, that we need a contrite spirit only when we first repent and believe in the Lord, or when we subsequently fall into sin. We should know, however, that God looks in us for a state of contrition at all times. Even if we do not sin daily, we are none the less required by Him to be of a humble spirit, remembering that we have a sinful nature that may be stirred up again at any moment.

The fact that as believers we have been joined to the Lord in one spirit does not mean that forever afterwards we are infallible. As we come to know ourselves, we realize how undependable are our ideas, how treacherous our feelings and desires. We dare not trust ourselves, but acknowledge that unless sustained by God we will certainly fall. This is contrition of spirit. With this man God dwells.

MAY 22

"The Spirit himself beareth witness with our spirit, that we are children of God." Romans 8:16

A man's regeneration can never be produced by the activities of his soul. To be penitent, to express sorrow for sin, even with tears, and then to make a decision for Christ do not in themselves save a man. Confession, decision, or any other religious act must not be construed as producing new birth.

Rational judgment, intellectual understanding, mental acceptance, the pursuit of the good and true—all these are excellent activities of man's soul. They may bring him to the point of hunger for God. But although they may function as servants, man's ideas and feelings and choices cannot hold office as masters. In this matter of salvation, their role is only secondary. The biblical reality of new birth belongs to a deeper realm. It is nothing less than the awakening of divine life in a man's spirit through the entry of the Holy Spirit of God.

MAY 23

"He sent a man before them; Joseph was sold for a servant." Psalm 105:17

Of the many typical servants of God in the Old Testament, Joseph is perhaps the most perfect. Yet while the Scripture reveals no apparent flaw in his character, we know well that his was no easy pathway. From a comparatively early age, his life was a series of bitter trials. He was the victim of much injustice. In spite of his faithfulness, he was dogged by one trouble after another.

When did his troubles begin? Surely with his dreams. In them he saw what God was going to do and recognized his own place in God's plan. It was his dreams that started things off. They represent spiritual vision. By them he saw what his brothers could not see. "This dreamer cometh," they said, and hated him. But because he saw, Joseph could stand fast through all those grim experiences, and by him God was able to fulfill His plan for His earthly people.

✑

MAY 24

"Casting down imaginations, and every high thing that is exalted against the knowledge of God."
2 Corinthians 10:5

One sphere of Satan's operations is man's thought life. He arouses imaginations which must first be suppressed before we can bring our thoughts into captivity to the obedience of Christ. We need to know what satanic temptation is. The devil will inject into your mind a thought, a fancy, which appears to be your own. Attracted by it, you accept and use it as though it were yours, though in actual origin it is his.

Many sins are first committed in the mind's imagination. Many unpleasantnesses among Christian brothers and sisters arise from fancies. As Martin Luther suggested, "You cannot forbid a bird from flying over your head, but you can prevent it from making a nest in your hair." Refuse to let evil thoughts find a resting place in you.

◈

MAY 25

"My meat is to do the will of him that sent me, and to accomplish his work." John 4:34

A wonderful feature of spiritual ministry is that it refreshes the one who engages in it. Take, for example, the incident of Jesus at the well of Sychar. He was genuinely thirsty when He asked the woman for a drink, but in His concern for her as a needy sinner He ignored His own condition. Instead He engaged her in a conversation that ministered the Water of Life to her soul.

Then the disciples returned. To their surprise, the Lord looked so refreshed that they began to ask one another where this provision had come from. The answer was, of course, that in giving another to drink of the living water, He Himself had found His own thirst satisfied. Life in the Spirit and ministry in the Spirit are always like this.

MAY 26

"There was given to me a thorn in the flesh, a messenger of Satan to buffet me." 2 Corinthians 12:7

The amazing fact apparent in the Bible is that it is relatively easy for a "heathen" to be healed, but that healing for a Christian is not as easy. The New Testament overwhelmingly shows us that whenever an unbeliever came to Jesus for healing, he was cured immediately. Now the gift of healing is surely for the Christian no less than for the unbeliever; yet the Bible tells of believers who were not healed. Among these are some of the most godly—Trophimus, Timothy, and Paul. Each of these three excellent brothers in Christ had to endure sickness.

It is clear that sickness is different from sin in its outworking. Sin does not produce any fruit of holiness, whereas sickness does. Do not look upon sickness or pain as something terrible. In whose hand is the knife? Remember that it is in God's hand. Why should we be anxious over infirmity, as though it were in the control of the enemy? Without God's permission Satan can make no one sick. All infirmities are measured to us by God for the sake of the enrichment they can bring.

MAY 27

"Now ye are the body of Christ, and severally members thereof." 1 Corinthians 12:27

The living consciousness of our fellowship in Christ is a very precious thing. It awakens in us a growing and deepening sense of "belonging." The nature of the butterfly, always "going it alone," gives place to the nature of the bee, always operating from the hive, always working, not for itself, but for the whole. It means that we see our own standing before God, not as isolated units but as members one of another.

Units have no special use, exercise limited ministry, and can easily be overlooked or left out. Whether we are present or not is no one's concern. A unit scarcely affects even statistics. But members are otherwise. They cannot be passive in the Body; they dare not merely stand looking on. None of them can ever say, "I don't count."

MAY 28

"Resist the devil, and he will flee from you." James 4:7

A child of God must not be inordinately curious. There are byways he need not explore, where Satan stands ready to entice the inquisitive with false information. At first the Christian may be attracted to such knowledge as beneficial, but unless these dangerous thoughts are cut off at the outset they will get out of hand afterwards. We must resist all vain speculations.

When such a thought has once been resisted in Jesus' name, the matter is completely closed. Should the thought return a second time, it may be ignored. Resist the devil once, and the promise is that he will flee. You should believe what God says, that Satan has fled away. You need not resist him again, for to do so is to discredit the first resistance. Each new resistance means deeper distrust of God's word, until you become occupied with "resisting Satan" from dawn to dusk. The more you think about it, the more confused will you become. No! Simply turn away to Jesus and forget all else.

MAY 29

"And he made us to be a kingdom, to be priests unto his God and Father." Revelation 1:6

At Sinai God told the people of Israel that He would set them up as a kingdom of priests. China is a nation of etiquette and India of philosophy, but Israel's role was unique. Everyone, man or woman, adult or child, was to be a priest toward God and toward mankind. Because of their failure, however, what was intended for the whole nation of Israel had to be reserved for the tribe of Levi.

Now, through Christ, the promise has been restored. His Church in the world is a kingdom of priests. Under the Old Covenant all who were disabled, lame, or blemished were barred from priestly service; but today, we, the base, the unclean, the blind and crippled, are called by God to be priests. With the New Covenant, the voice from heaven comes to tell us that all saved ones are chosen to serve Him and doing so, to draw mankind back to Him.

MAY 30

"Friendship of the world is enmity with God."
James 4:4

Notice what this statement says. It does not suggest that we should treat the people of the world as enemies. Jesus never made hostility to the world a condition for loving Him. It does mean, though, that when you become a believer, former deep friendships and intimate relationships can no longer exist exactly as they did before. You may still love a former friend, but your desire now is to win him to Christ. You may go out to him, but with the new purpose of sharing with him the good news that has brought you such release. This is what Cornelius did in inviting his relatives and close friends to his home to hear Peter speak.

Tell your former friends what has happened. Tell them you have believed in the Lord Jesus. Should they react unfavorably, know that it is better to be unwelcomed than to be drawn by them away from the Lord. If possible maintain some association, for this is good, but do not crave for intimate friendship. You belong to the Lord Jesus and are there to represent Him. Sooner or later you will see them either turn to Him themselves or forsake you. Rarely is it any other way.

MAY 31

"And Moses made haste, and bowed his head toward the earth, and worshipped." Exodus 34:8

Moses first worships, then he prays. He first acknowledges the rightness of God's ways, and then he seeks God's grace. Unlike us, he does not at once beseech God, on the ground of His grace, to reverse His decision. We are always trying to persuade God to change His way of working. Without considering His ways, we just open our lips and ask Him to remove the pressure here, the sickness there, the domestic problems elsewhere. To pray after this fashion is not to worship God.

We have lost sight of our place before God. We are making ourselves too big. Moses was not like that. Before he prayed, he first acknowledged God's sovereignty and, with bowed head, accepted His ways. Thereafter he prayed that if he had found grace in God's sight, God would still go up in the midst of His people. The acceptance of God's ways does not rule out prayer nor eliminate grace. But there is an order here: we first capitulate to God, then we pray to Him. Prayer may be the expression of my will; worship precedes it, and is the acceptance of the will of God.

&

JUNE 1

"Make full my joy, that ye be of the same mind."
Philippians 2:2

I would like to point out that this request for the saints to be like-minded is not addressed to the universal Church. Though the universal Church can learn from it, the words apply especially to the Philippians to whom Paul wrote this letter. You Christians in Philippi, you Philippian brothers, you are the ones who must be like-minded.

It is not nearly so important for you who love the Lord here in Foochow to be like-minded with the brothers of the church in Shanghai, or with the brothers of the church in Lanchou. What is of major importance is like-mindedness with those here in this city. This is what the Bible commands. If this is lacking in your own locality, all your doctrines are but fanciful ideals.

~

"And Moses cried unto Jehovah, saying, Heal her, O God, I beseech Thee." Numbers 12:13

When Miriam and Aaron combined to challenge Moses' unique position, no words of self-vindication came from the lips of God's servant. He had nothing to say in his own defense. During the whole affair, he acted as though he were scarcely more than a spectator. He had no personal axe to grind; he neither reproved nor argued.

Moreover, he quickly forgave and was ready enough to pray for Miriam when she needed his prayers. Had he not tasted God's mercy he would have said to Aaron, "Why do you not pray to God yourself, since you insist that God speaks to you also?" But, like Christ who prayed for His captors, he readily pleaded for Miriam's recovery. In this he shows us the way to fulfill the command "Do good to them that hate you; pray for them that despitefully use you."

JUNE 3

"Ye know that your labor is not vain in the Lord."
1 Corinthians 15:58

If our work for God is truly accomplished in His strength, it cannot but bring results. Yet supposing we have been commissioned by Him and have labored for eight or ten years without seeing any results at all, can we continue to toil on faithfully, simply because God has commanded it? How many of us are prepared to serve solely because it is God's command? Or how many work for the sake of seeing fruit?

Since God's work is eternal in nature, He seeks men with faith to labor for Him. It is difficult for us humans who live in time to perceive and understand the work of God, by reason of its eternal character. But it helps to remember that the work of the Lord Jesus was that of the cross—losing for the sake of greater gain. Exactly so is the work of the Christian to be. Today God needs followers who will travail with Him to the end, whether or not they see results.

JUNE 4

*"Who is this that cometh up from the wilderness,
leaning upon her beloved?" Song of Songs 8:5*

The Holy Spirit draws our attention to this surprising sight, which is none other than the mystery of the Church. She has the world behind her, for she is coming away from the wilderness; and she is making an upward movement, for she is advancing toward a heavenly goal. What is more, she is utterly dependent, leaning hard upon her Beloved. She knows herself to be incapable of finding her own paths out of this wilderness world, so she must keep close to him. And her dependence and nearness are not a matter of duty or fear so much as of heart love.

So we have a glimpse of the onward and upward movement of the pilgrim Church which has an "on-high" calling in Christ. Why should we wait for the Lord's return in passive contemplation? It is spiritual fitness which makes us ready for His coming, and that demands an onward progress with Him now.

JUNE 5

"Ye have not yet resisted unto blood, striving against sin." Hebrews 12:4

What is the meaning of Christian suffering? Unless we are called to martyrdom, our resisting and striving against sin has not reached the point of bloodshed. Nevertheless, we still deplore our lot. Do we expect to have a prosperous road in this life—to wear a white linen garment and walk leisurely on a golden street leading to a pearly gate?

God has arranged all kinds of environment, all sorts of happenings, and many sufferings, all with a view to creating in each of His children a certain character which will glorify Him. To be scourged may be the evidence of His approval. Chastisement is love's arrangement. Love measures and love plans. God may not deal thus with everyone, but He certainly does so with those whom He has accepted as sons.

JUNE 6

"What doth Jehovah require of thee, but to do justly, and to love kindness, and to walk humbly with thy God?" Micah 6:8

Humility is a grace that should genuinely move people, but the way some of us Christians parade our humility reveals plainly the falsity of our hearts. We talk endlessly of being humble, but only display thereby what Paul calls a "voluntary humility" (Colossians 2:18), having hidden motives and not the genuine article. It were really better to call it pride!

He who is truly humble is not like that. He is real. He acts naturally and speaks gently. Like his master, he will "take a towel . . ." for he esteems others better than himself. He is not too proud, either, to ask for their help when he needs it. No wonder men ask one another, "Who is his Lord whom he serves so gladly?"

JUNE 7

"I have learned, in whatsoever state I am, therein to be content." Philippians 4:11

Paul was one who not only knew Christ, but had had Christ wrought into his very being through the testings of time. "I have learned," he says, and the context refers to experiences of physical want. Through such experiences, which took time, there was a progressive but a quite definite change in his character. And this is what we ourselves need; not only exchanged lives, where it is no longer I but Christ, but changed lives. Of course we cannot have the second without the first, but God does indeed want the second. He wants a real transformation in us.

Let us not misunderstand God's ways with us. If He uses special trials and testings, it is for a special purpose. A valuable vessel or a well-finished tool cannot be produced without a high price being paid. Only poor quality goods can be produced cheaply.

JUNE 8

"If any man love the world, the love of the Father is not in him." 1 John 2:15

Today the world comes and searches us out. There is a force abroad now which is captivating men. Did you ever feel the power of the world as you do today? Did you ever hear so much talk about money? Did you ever think so much about food and clothing? Wherever you go, even among Christians, the things of the world are the topic of conversation. The world has advanced to the very door of the Church and is seeking to draw God's people into its grasp. Never in this sphere of things have we so urgently needed to know the power of the cross to deliver us as we do at this present time.

Jesus spoke reassuringly to His disciples about this. He also prayed for them: "These are in the world, and I come to thee. Holy Father, keep them in Thy name." Ultimately when we touch the things of the world, the only question we need ask ourselves is, "How is this thing affecting my relationship with the Father?"

JUNE 9

"If Balak would give me his house full of silver and gold, I cannot go beyond the word of Jehovah."
Numbers 24:13

Only when the Word of God was voiced by Balaam did his words become a prophecy. He spoke as the Spirit of God came upon him and irrespective of his own moral condition, for he spoke in spite of himself. God was merely employing the man's mouth to utter His word. Had Balaam attempted to add his own thoughts and feelings, it would at once have ceased to be the Word of God.

How different is the way God's Word was proclaimed through the Lord Jesus! Earlier, God had engaged men's voices to propagate His word. Even John the Baptist, the last of the prophets, was but a voice in the wilderness. When we come to the Lord Jesus, however, His consistency of character compels us to speak of Him as the living Word of God. When He opened his mouth, there was God's Word; but even when He kept it shut, that Word was still living there in His wonderful Person.

JUNE 10

*"I John, your brother and partaker with you in the
tribulation and kingdom and patience which are
in Jesus . . ." Revelation 1:9*

In Revelation 6:10 we hear the cry "How long?"
Those who utter this plaint are finding it difficult to exercise patience any more. They cry for
vengeance, for the execution of judgment. Surely
if impatience is justified in any, it is justified in
the dead saints rather than the living, for they
have waited so much longer. Even so, they are
told that the time of patience has not yet expired.

It is significant that John calls himself a partaker in the patience of Jesus at the outset of a
book which deals so much with judgment. As
soon as judgment is carried out, there will be no
more need for patience. John, about to write on
the subject of judgment, declares that he is still
living in the realm of patience. When God pours
out His wrath upon the earth, then the time of
patience will be over. Meanwhile, He calls upon
His people to share with Him in it.

JUNE 11

*"Who shall lay anything to the charge of God's elect?
It is God that justifieth." Romans 8:33*

To repent for sin is good, but to become engrossed with the thought of our own evil is wrong because we too easily mistake this for Christian humility, not realizing that we are but suffering the harmful effects of Satan's accusations. Of course it is true that when we sin, we must confess it and deal with it. But there is another lesson which we must learn. It is to look, not upon ourselves, but upon the Lord Jesus.

Once a child of God accepts Satan's accusations, all day long he will feel that he is wrong. From morning till evening, whether working, resting, walking, reading the Scriptures, or praying, he will be consumed with the thought of his own worthlessness. The Word of God tells us that the blood of Jesus, God's Son, cleanses us from all sin—and "all sin" means any sin, whether it be great or small.

JUNE 12

*"Wherefore let us keep the feast . . . with the
unleavened bread of sincerity and truth."*
1 Corinthians 5:8

The breaking of the bread has two meanings
in Scripture: one is to remember the Lord
and the other is to express fellowship with all
the children of God. It is literally impossible for
me to give the right hand of fellowship to every
one of God's children here on earth. Yet on the
Lord's Day His people touch symbolically the
same bread, as they break it in His name here
and therefore throughout all the earth.

Wherever they may be, they touch by faith
the same living Bread as I. So in this way I relate
by touch with all the true children of God. Here
I meet all my brothers and sisters, as well as my
Lord. I not only have fellowship with those who
share the bread with me in my local meeting,
but also with all whose hands are outstretched
to touch the same Bread of Life throughout the
world. We, though so many and so different, are
yet one loaf in Christ.

❧

JUNE 13

"We departed, and went on our journey; and they all,
with wives and children, brought us on our way."
Acts 21:5

I trust that if the Lord is gracious to our churches today, half of the people added to them
will be the children of Christian parents and
the other half will be people rescued from the
world. The gospel does indeed rescue people
from the world, but a church cannot be strong
if the increase comes only from that quarter and
not also from the children of its members. We
should hope to see a steady flow coming also
from Christian families. People such as Timothy
must be brought in through the influence of a
Lois and a Eunice. Thereby will the church be
greatly enriched.

To lead your children to God, you must
yourself walk ahead and let them follow. The
standard of faith which you pursue will contribute largely toward theirs.

JUNE 14

"As many as I love, I reprove and chasten."
Revelation 3:19

How different were these Christians at Laodicea from those whom the Lord recognized as truly rich at Smyrna. The Laodiceans may well have been marvelous Christians with much of which to be proud, but it would have been better if they had not themselves boasted of it but had left it to others to applaud them.

Spiritual things are not to be boasted of. One can boast of worldly riches, and the paper money will not fly away unspent nor will the amount magically decrease, but the spiritual riches you boast of vanish with the telling. When a Christian says he is strong, at that moment his strength has gone. If the face of a Moses really shines, he is never the one to be aware of it. We always hope that we are growing spiritually, but it is not for us to appraise our own progress.

"Moab hath been at ease from his youth, and he hath settled on his lees, and hath not been emptied from vessel to vessel . . . therefore his taste remaineth in him, and his scent is not changed." Jeremiah 48:11

The imagery of this verse needs explaining. In wine that is settling on its lees (that which settles during fermentation), stationary and still, the upper level becomes clear; but beneath is a bitter sediment that will muddy it again if shaken. Before the days of filters, to clear the wine it was emptied carefully from one vessel to another, but however skillfully this was done some of the lees would get across. So the process must be repeated again and again to rid it of its unwelcome taste.

Moab, Israel's natural cousins, had escaped that treatment; had not, as Israel had, been sifted and purified through afflictions, with the result, God says, that her bitter taste still clung. There is thus value in God's discipline of us, a little today and a little more tomorrow. The goal is a savor in us, a character that meets with His approval, delights His heart.

"If any man's work shall abide which he built thereon, he shall receive a reward." 1 Corinthians 3:14

We will better understand the meaning of this trial by fire if we remember that the words "as a flame of fire" describe the eyes of the risen Christ. At the future judgment He will search our work with His own discerning light, and we can be sure that His standards are absolute. That is why we ourselves now come daily to the light of God to test that our work is being "wrought in God."

Whether or not we receive the Lord's praise in the future depends on how we please Him in doing His will today. Of course, our reward is a small matter; the real purpose of us all is to satisfy His heart. I believe that every saved person shares the same desire to bring pleasure to the Lord. That way the judgment seat becomes a goal before us that is full of the promise of His approval.

JUNE 17

"I give my judgment, as one that hath obtained mercy of the Lord to be trustworthy." 1 Corinthians 7:25

God does not want the man He creates to be like a machine, having no freedom of choice, but having to obey perfectly. It would be easy for him to make such a machine. There would be no trouble with man, but neither would there be glory for God. Such obedience and goodness have no spiritual value. There may not be any fault or sin, yet neither can there be holiness, for the obedience is passive. God rejects such a thing.

God does not want an automaton; He wants a man with a free will. It is a calculated risk with God to choose man as a minister of the Word. Yet in spite of the complexity of man and his many problems of sin and weakness, God entrusts His Word to man. Through the greatest rigor God obtains the highest glory.

JUNE 18

"Rest in Jehovah, and wait patiently for him."
Psalm 37:7

One who is at rest in God is not easily excited by outward stresses. His inner strength is what allays his anxieties and troubles of mind. To each hurricane there is an eye. At the circumference the wind whirls violently, but the eye, deep at the center, is most calm.

The Lord Jesus was never put off balance by outside influences. Even at the last, when a band of soldiers came to seize Him with torches and weapons, He stepped forward and asked them whom they were seeking. Being told that they sought Jesus of Nazareth, He calmly answered, "I am He." Met by Him thus, they retreated and fell to the ground. Those who would seize Him were terrified of the One to be seized, whereas the external stresses had no power to move Him. At the center of His being, the eye of the storm, He was at rest with God.

"Whom have I in heaven but thee? And there is none upon earth that I desire besides thee." Psalm 73:25

I cannot sufficiently stress the importance of loving the Lord with our whole heart. God calls for no less than this. He is unwilling to share our hearts with anyone or anything else. Even should He receive the biggest share, He is still not well pleased. He asks us to love Him totally.

God does not tolerate competition. Our all must be on the altar. This is the Christian's way to spiritual power. And shortly after the sacrifice is laid on the altar—nay, after the last sacrifice is duly placed there—fire will come down from heaven. Without the altar, there will be no heavenly fire. Neither our mental understanding of the cross of Christ nor our endless talk about it will give us the power of the Holy Spirit. Only our laying everything on the altar for love of Him will do that.

❧

JUNE 20

"Be ye transformed by the renewing of your mind."
Romans 12:2

This verse lays special emphasis on the mind. It is possible for a child of God to have a new life and a new heart, but to be without a new head. The heart may be full of love, while the mind remains totally lacking in perception of divine things. In his degenerate state man had a darkened mind and one that was at enmity with God. God must therefore alter man's mind if He would impart life to him, and so the original definition of repentance is none other than "a change of mind."

After conversion, however, the intents of the heart will be pure and yet the thoughts of the head may still be confused. Intellectual doubts may remain to be resolved. If a Christian's mind is not progressively renewed, his life is bound to be unbalanced. Undeniably life is more important than knowledge; yet for growth in life it is essential to seek knowledge, and for this our daily standard of truth is God's Word.

JUNE 21

"And this is life eternal, that they should know thee the only true God, and him whom thou didst send, even Jesus Christ." John 17:3

The eternal life which we secure by believing does indeed relate to future blessing, but it also has a meaning for us today. This life constitutes here and now an introduction to God through His Son Jesus Christ. Without it, no amount of mental exercise can equip us to know God. We may reason about Him, we may familiarize ourselves with the Bible and its teachings, we may even labor zealously for Him in some field of service, but not until we accept life eternal as His gift will we discover and enjoy personal knowledge of Him.

Faith in human ideals is no substitute for knowing God in our spirits. To believe on the Lord Jesus is to enter into eternal life as a present reality and to discover thereby a knowledge of the true God that we never possessed before.

JUNE 22

"But far be it from me to glory, save in the cross of our Lord Jesus Christ, through which the world hath been crucified unto me." Galatians 6:14

When God comes to you and me with the revelation of the finished work of Christ, he does not only show us ourselves crucified with Christ on the cross. He shows us our world there too. If you and I cannot escape the judgment of the cross, then neither can the world escape that judgment. When I see this, I do not try to repudiate a world I love; I see that the cross has repudiated it. I do not try to escape a world that clings to me; I see that by the cross I have escaped.

Let me ask you: What is your occupation? A merchant? A doctor? A farmer? Do not run away from these callings. Physical separation from the world does not bring about spiritual separation; and the reverse is also true, that physical contact with the world does not necessitate spiritual capture by the world. Eden was a garden without an artificial wall to keep Satan out. God intended that Adam and Eve should "guard it" by themselves constituting a moral barrier to the enemy. Today, through Christ, God plans in the hearts of His redeemed people an

Eden in which, in triumphant fact, Satan will at last have no moral access whatever.

❧

JUNE 23

"All the saints salute you." 2 Corinthians 13:13

It is futile to seek to produce individual saints. Praise the Lord that individual sinners are saved, but this is that they may become members of Christ's Body. God is never satisfied with single, separate Christians. The divine goal is one Man, and not a host of small men. The cross and resurrection point us forward to the Body.

This must be put into practice. Just as reading a book about London is no substitution for visiting the city, and just as having a cookbook full of recipes is valueless until we go into the kitchen, so it is not enough that we believe what we are taught about the Body of Christ. It is essential that we learn and practice our holiness together with other believers. We have to renounce purely individual goals and learn to move with others and wait for others. Often we shall find this means not only adding to us what is of Christ by the Spirit, but also subtracting painfully whatever in us needs to be put away by the cross. But painful or not, let us practice our membership of the Body.

❧

JUNE 24

"And the three mighty men brake through the host of the Philistines, and drew water out of the well of Bethlehem." 2 Samuel 23:16

There is an aspect of suffering referred to in God's Word in which it is seen as the deliberate choice of His children, those whose consuming desire it is to be of service to Him. This is not something imposed upon them to which they reluctantly submit, but something they joyfully choose. David's mighty men need not have exposed themselves to danger in this way, but when they heard him express his longing, they hazarded their lives to satisfy it.

The Christian should have a mind to suffer hardship. God will put a limit to our sufferings, but there should be no limit to our willingness to suffer for His testimony and for the salvation of men. This mind to suffer is not a sentimental idea; it is the virile spirit of those who disregard careful calculations and the crippling fear of going to extremes, all for love of Christ.

JUNE 25

"Abide in me, and I in you. As the branch cannot bear fruit of itself, except it abide in the vine; so neither can ye, except ye abide in me." John 15:4

To abide means to stay where I am. It does not mean to get in or get out. I could not be asked to stay in if I were not already there. Christ never commanded me to get myself into Him. That is not my work, but God's. I cannot do it, however hard I try. He has placed me there. What He does command me to do is to take care that I do not get out.

The difficulty is that we are always prone to let ourselves be uprooted, and Satan is working unceasingly to shake us from our position in Christ. If we yield to some sense of failure, we imagine that we are out of Christ, and we tend to treat ourselves as though somehow we were displaced from Him. Yet even though we feel acutely that it is so, we must never allow ourselves to disbelieve God. He assures us that we are in Christ: all He asks us is that, in attitude and action as well as faith, we stay there.

JUNE 26

"Ye are God's husbandry." 1 Corinthians 3:9

The natural trend of things in this fallen world is always away from God. Suppose we take so apparently innocent a matter as agriculture. No one would suggest that in Eden, where the tree of life flourished, farming or gardening was wrong. It was God-appointed. But as soon as it was let go from under the hand of God, thistles grew. Man was condemned to an endless round of drudgery and disappointment, and an element of perversity marked the fruit of his toil. "Cursed is the ground for thy sake."

The deliverance of Noah was God's great movement of recovery, in which the earth was given a fresh start. But how swift, how tragic was man's reversion. "Noah began to be a husbandman . . . and he drank of the wine and was drunken." How different is the Church, God's husbandry! Through the grace of God she possesses an inherent life-power capable, if she responds to it, of keeping her constantly moving Godward, or of recalling her Godward if she strays.

JUNE 27

"And God said, Let us make man in our image, after our likeness: and let them have dominion . . . over all the earth." Genesis 1:26

Already in God's act of creation He makes known His desire that man should rule. Moreover, He marks out a specific area—namely, the earth—for His dominion. God's attention is focused upon this earth, which is destined to become the center of all problems.

The prayer which the Lord Jesus has taught us is also concerned with this earth. "When you pray, say: Our Father who art in heaven, Hallowed be Thy name. Thy kingdom come. Thy will be done, as in heaven, so on earth." In the original, the last phrase is common to all three clauses, not merely to the final one, so that the hallowing of His name, the coming of His kingdom, and the doing of His will are all "as in heaven, so on earth." In other words, there is no problem with heaven; the problem is with the earth, and it is for the earth that God contends. Shall we not, in prayer, exercise man's dominion by claiming this earth for God?

❧

JUNE 28

"If there be any virtue, and if there be any praise, think on these things." Philippians 4:8

The cause of much poverty of thought lies in thinking too extravagantly. Learn to conserve your thought, not waste it. Exercise your mind, but do not exhaust its energy on insignificant things. Are you studying the Bible? Do not dissipate your mental powers on minor difficulties of the text. When you know the Author Himself, it matters little whether you can explain these minor problems or not. Are you concerned with the spiritual life? Do not waste intellectual effort on spiritual problems. These are not solved by thinking, but by the entrance of God's light.

We must daily train ourselves in regard to our thoughts. Do not imagine that God wishes to eliminate reason, but realize that He only desires to bring our thoughts into captivity to the obedience of Christ.

❧

JUNE 29

"And he that is of a cool spirit is a man of understanding." Proverbs 17:27

Our spirit needs to be fervent, yet also to be cool. Fervency is related to diligence in the service of the Lord, whereas coolness is related to knowledge. If the Christian would simply bear in mind that God cannot lead anyone who is in turmoil, he might be spared many errors.

Never decide on any course or start to do anything while emotion is agitating like a roaring sea. It is in times of emotional upheaval that mistakes are readily made. The mind is easily affected by feelings, and with a restless mind how can we distinguish between right and wrong? As emotion pulsates, the understanding becomes deceived and even conscience is rendered unreliable. Decisions made in such circumstances are likely afterwards to be regretted. Cultivate a cool spirit. You will open the way for God to give you understanding.

JUNE 30

"If there is therefore any exhortation in Christ, if any consolation of love . . . if any tender mercies and compassions." Philippians 2:1

How timely here are the words "in Christ." Suppose that Paul had exhorted his brothers in Philippi to be united in love and mercy and compassion; they could well have answered that although such unity was desirable, they could never attain to it. They each had their own goals and ideals and interests. How could they ever expect to abandon them and be so united?

Paul, however, began by stressing the power that there is in Christ. Outside of Him they would of course be defeated, but because they were in Christ they could draw freely on the resources which are found in Him. If in Him there were no mercy and compassion, these virtues would be impossible to find in His people. They are found in Christ, however, and thus provide, for all His own, the source and the nutrient of a life poured out in His service.

≈

JULY 1

"Then Job arose, and rent his robe, and shaved his head, and fell down upon the ground, and worshipped." Job 1:20

In the mystery of His ways God permitted Job to be deprived of everything he possessed, though He Himself had just borne witness of him that there was "none like him in the earth, a perfect and an upright man." Four messengers had arrived almost simultaneously with the news that within the compass of one short day, he had been stripped of everything he possessed. How did he react? He fell down before God and worshiped.

Where there is true worship, there are no complaints. Here was a man so utterly subject to God that he could unhesitatingly bow to all His ways. Let us cease questioning God's dealings with us, and with our brothers and sisters, however baffling they may be. Let us cease asking Him for explanations and in simplicity accept that His thoughts are higher than our thoughts and all His ways are perfect.

JULY 2

"If so be that ye heard him." Ephesians 4:21

After I was saved, I used to feel dissatisfied with Peter's sermon on the Day of Pentecost. It did not, I thought, make things clear at all, for there is nothing in it about the plan of salvation. How strange that Peter did not even use the title "Savior"! But nevertheless, what was the result? The people, we are told, were pricked in their hearts and cried, "What shall we do?" Again, to Cornelius Peter only spoke about who Christ was; he gave no explanation of the meaning of His death. Yet even so, the Holy Spirit fell upon them all.

The great weakness of present preaching of the gospel is that we try to make people understand the plan of salvation, or we try to drive people to the Lord through fear of sin and its consequences. Wherein have we failed? I am sure that it is in this, that our hearers do not see him. They only see "sin" or "salvation," whereas their need is to see the Lord Jesus and touch Him.

JULY 3

"They gave him wine to drink mingled with gall: and when he had tasted it, he would not drink."
Matthew 27:34

To condemn a man to the cross was to condemn him to an agonizing death, but it was permitted to alleviate the sufferings of the crucified by offering a drink of gall mixed with wine or vinegar. No doubt the slightest alleviation of his pain was welcomed by the condemned. Our Lord, however, was an exception. When He tasted the drink that was lifted to His lips, He refused it. There was nothing in Him that cried out for the easing of His pain.

We profess to bear the cross, but how eager we are to drink that wine mingled with gall! May we awake to the truth that if we are yearning for an anodyne, we are not truly bearing the cross of Christ. Only those who find their trials irksome need a soothing draught. How we love sympathy! We have an insatiable craving to be comforted, seeking it from every possible source and feeling aggrieved if it is not offered to us. Unwittingly we reveal that we know little of His cross, which involves a joyful acceptance of the will of God.

"That he might sanctify it, having cleansed it by the washing of water with the word." Ephesians 5:26

God's highest revelation of the Church is seen in this letter. Its outstanding feature is that it starts, not with sinners being saved, but with their having been chosen in Christ. Thus in Ephesians something transcendent is unveiled to us. We see the Church, chosen in Christ before the foundation of the world, formed out from Him, and destined forever to manifest His glory.

At the same time, however, Ephesians shows us that man's sin and man's fall are facts. Every one of us who belongs to Christ possesses a new spirit which is truly of Him, but alongside this there are still in us many things which are not of Christ. That is why we are told in this verse about Christ's activities to cleanse us. He wants to restore us till we completely match with God's eternal design. It is true, therefore, that God plans to bring us to the place where cleansing is no longer necessary, but today we still need to be cleansed.

JULY 5

"Are ye so foolish? having begun in the Spirit, are ye now perfected in the flesh?" Galatians 3:3

Paul makes it clear in his letter to the Romans that the sinner depends on the grace of God for his salvation. In Galatians he shows us that the believer depends equally upon that grace for his continuance in the Christian life. We never did anything, or gave God anything, for our salvation, and this must be the basis of our walk with Him.

God begins by giving us a new position so that we have a new start. If I am down at the bottom of a pit, then I continue there with no way of getting out of it until God lifts me out and puts me upon a rock. He does this by placing me in Christ. By doing so He has settled all my past. But He has gone further than that. By placing the life of Christ within me, He has given me all I need for the present and for the entire future. Spiritual progress, then, is not by an agonizing striving to attain, but by looking trustfully to God's grace and continuing to receive of Christ's fullness.

JULY 6

"O ye that love Jehovah, hate evil." Psalm 97:10

Before ever we discuss the subject of deliverance from sin, we must first mention a condition or qualification of those who are to be delivered. Even though God's deliverance is prepared for all, not all are delivered. The Apostle Paul indicates this almost unconsciously in Romans 7. In the experience described there, he finally becomes emancipated because he has fulfilled the condition of knowing what to hate as well as what to desire.

We read not only how he gets released, but also how he feels in his heart before he is released: "For not what I would, that do I practice; but what I hate, that I do" (Romans 7:15). Hence the first and foremost question today is: Do you love what you are doing now, or do you hate it? The apostle was so unwilling to live a life in sin that he was determined to get out of it. It was due to his hatred of it and his determination to find an escape that he found deliverance.

JULY 7

"I sat down under his shadow with great delight, and his fruit was sweet to my taste." Song of Songs 2:3

To the true believer, the love of Christ is all-sufficient. In it the Christian finds rest, protection, and satisfaction. The singer of this song has told of running after her beloved, but now she exclaims with joy that she has come to rest. Like a tree, his shadow is over her and his fruit gives her deep satisfaction.

No noonday heat can penetrate, no fever exhaust the one who flees to Christ for shelter. As he comes to rest beneath the ever green coolness of the Savior's love, he finds only "great delight" and a marvelous uplift of spirit. Moreover, he is not only protected from the scorching heat of circumstances, he is inwardly refreshed. There are some trees which, though always green, do not bear fruit; but Christ is the unique tree of life. At one and the same time He affords shade from the burning heat of the day and satisfying fruit for our inward sustenance.

JULY 8

*"From a babe thou hast known the sacred writings
which are able to make thee wise unto salvation."*
2 Timothy 3:15

One way of leading children to the Lord is an effective "family altar." In Genesis, the tent and the altar were closely associated. In other words, worship and the family are connected. This is why family prayer and Bible reading together are so indispensable today. Parents must lead their children in simplicity, not just praying for them but with them, and also teaching each child how to pray for himself.

In a family gathering, the children must be the first consideration. Family worship can be a failure because it is too long or too profound. The exposition must be on the children's level, not that of the parents, who can worship and be taught in the church. Prayer with them must be in words and ideas they can understand. We must try to attract the children to Christ and let their response to Him be spontaneous. Always let them feel they matter to God.

JULY 9

"Behold, here is thy pound, which I kept laid up in a napkin." Luke 19:20

Napkins or handkerchiefs should be used for wiping off the sweat of toil. No one's napkin should be misapplied to the wrapping up of his talent. Whether a church can grow prevailingly does not depend on whether or not those who receive five talents, or ten, come forth and serve. The weight of responsibility for growth rests on those with one talent. If the one-talented are employed and growing, all in the church will be well; but if they bury their talent, then the whole church stagnates.

Thus we have only one hope; namely, that the weight of emphasis in every local church should be placed, not on those who are especially qualified, but on those less-gifted ones whom men despise. You have to tell them that God approves of their wiping off the perspiration of honest work for Him, and that without it that work will not be done.

JULY 10

"But Christ is all, and in all." Colossians 3:11

The Body of Christ is not Jew and Greek, barbarian and Scythian, but one new man, without national distinctions. The following story is a good illustration. After the First World War, some Christian brothers from England went to Germany to attend a conference. One of the brothers in Germany rose to introduce the visitors, saying, "Now that the war is over, we have some English brothers visiting us, to whom we extend our warmest welcome."

Among those introduced, one stood up and replied, "We are not English brothers, but brothers from England." How well spoken were those words! For remember, even in the church in Jerusalem this mistake began to be made when a dispute arose between the Hebrews and the Grecians (Acts 6). It is good that at Antioch the disciples came to be called Christians, for in the Church there is neither national distinction nor racial difference, but only Christ who is all and in all. How satisfactory this is!

JULY 11

"And it came to pass, when the days were well-nigh come that he should be received up, he steadfastly set his face to go to Jerusalem." Luke 9:51

Nothing could sidetrack Christ from the goal; yet on His road thither He visited many cities and villages and taught in them. Without deviating from His course, He nevertheless bought up every opportunity by the way. Yes, though the hour approached when He "should be received up" to the Father, the short space of time between was filled with purposeful activity.

If we hope soon to be "received up" to meet Him, let us not spend the in-between time idly waiting for that day. Let me ask you: is this hope of His return just a part of our creed, or are we positively waiting for its realization? And what are we doing in the meantime? Are we daily walking with Him in the way of the cross? Are we telling those we encounter by the way the Good News of His salvation? And are we alone in our witness, or are we drawing others to labor with us? The goal is clear, but the road between is strewn with opportunities, if only we will set ourselves to do diligently all that comes to our hand.

JULY 12

"This is my beloved Son: hear ye him." Mark 9:7

We need God's Book and we need God's prophets. He would not have us discard either Moses or Elijah and what they represent. But the lesson of this incident on the Mount of Transfiguration is surely that neither of these can take the place of the living voice of God to our hearts.

The kingdom involves on the positive side a recognition of the absolute authority of Christ, and on the negative side a repudiation of every authority but His as final. It demands a firsthand intelligence of the will of God that embraces other God-given aids, but does not end with them. In the kingdom there is only one Voice to be heard, through whatever medium it speaks. Christianity is not independent of men and books—far from it. But the way of the kingdom is that the beloved Son speaks to me personally and directly, and that personally and directly I hear Him.

JULY 13

"But his wife looked back from behind him, and she became a pillar of salt." Genesis 19:26

It is possible for a believer outwardly to forsake the world, leaving everything behind, and yet inwardly to cling to those very elements which he has forsaken for Christ's sake. Just to cast back longing glances is proof enough of how easy it would be to go back and repossess what had once been given up.

That is why Jesus gave His strong admonition to His disciples that they should remember Lot's wife. She was one who did not forget her former possessions even in a time of great peril. We are not told that she was guilty of retracing a single step toward Sodom. All that she did was to look back. How revealing, though, was that backward glance! The question at issue is always, on what is my heart fixed?

JULY 14

"What I have, that I give thee. In the name of Jesus Christ of Nazareth, walk." Acts 3:6

What would we have done if confronted with the kind of need which faced Peter and John as this lame man made his appeal? Probably we would have brought the matter to a prayer meeting and urged one another to pray for this needy soul. The apostles did not do this. The words which they spoke were directed to the man himself—they were the words of testimony.

We may perhaps suggest that there are two elements in prayer. Prayer is certainly toward God, but it is sometimes also a matter of saying to this mountain, "Be thou removed!" There is tremendous power in Spirit-given witness addressed directly to the situation, as the book of the Acts so clearly shows.

JULY 15

"In whom ye also are builded together for a habitation of God in the Spirit." Ephesians 2:22

I was once told of a sister in Christ who was so quiet and gentle that she was "highly spiritual." "Who is she spiritual with?" I asked my informant. The revealing reply was, "Well, singers who can sing such high notes as she can, find few who can sing with them."

Alas, she was so spiritual that no one could be her spiritual companion! Such a sister is alright for display purposes, but she is no use for church building. The kind of Christian needed in the Church of God is one who can have another placed behind her and another in front, another over her and yet another under her, and still be spiritual. God did not just plan for a display of precious stones; He wanted a house.

"It is eleven days' journey from Horeb by the way of mount Seir unto Kadesh-barnea." Deuteronomy 1:2

Kadesh-barnea was at the very entry to the land of Canaan itself. Thus only eleven days after leaving Mount Sinai, the children of Israel would have entered Canaan. Yet because of their unbelief, they wandered in the wilderness for thirty-eight long years before their descendants finally entered the land. What a circuit they had traveled!

How many days have we wasted in our spiritual journey? All too many, I fear. Problems that might have been solved in a few days remain outstanding, often for years. Like the Israelites, we circle around in the wilderness, wasting God's time and our own. Instead let us heed His voice exhorting us to hold fast the beginning of our confidence firm to the end. His ways are straightforward. He has a promised rest for us to enter.

JULY 17

"The people sat down to eat and to drink, and rose up to play." Exodus 32:6

When God chose Israel to be his people, his plan was that they should be a kingdom of priests to himself. Now, however, they were worshiping an idol of their own choice and design. Their happiness lay in the fact that they could see this god which Aaron had cast of molten gold. The God whom Moses had led them to know had the great disadvantage of being invisible, and now even Moses himself was not to be found. It was very much easier for them to worship the golden calf standing there, familiar in form, in full view before them.

They now had another god and another worship. Whereas God had intended them to be His priests, they had turned themselves into priests of the calf. Man's attitude of independence always leads him to prefer a god of his own making. He likes to worhip what he can see and manipulate. It is much harder to submit to the authority of his faithful, unseen Creator.

JULY 18

"Whom he called, them he also justified: and whom he justified, them he also glorified." Romans 8:30

According to this Scripture, all who have been called and justified have already been glorified. The goal is attained. The Church has already come to glory. The ultimate reality is before God all the time. He sees the Church utterly pure, utterly perfect.

Spiritual growth is not so much a question of pressing through to some far-off and abstract goal, as of seeing God's ultimate standard in heaven and living in the power of that reality. Spiritual progress comes by finding out what you really are, not by trying to be what you hope to become. As we move forward to the basis of God's eternal facts, we shall see, here and now, the progressive manifestation of those facts in Christian lives.

JULY 19

"He rested on the seventh day from all His work which He had made." Genesis 2:2

Rest comes after work. Moreover, work must be completed to entire satisfaction before there can be true rest. God did not rest in the first six days, but He rested on the seventh. During the six days of creation, there were light, air, grass, herbs, and trees; there were the sun, the moon, and the stars; there were fish, birds, cattle, and creeping things. Finally there was man, and God rested from all His work. When God gained a man, he was satisfied.

"Behold, it was very good" (Genesis 1:31). Note the use of the word "behold." When we have purchased or produced an object with which we are particularly satisfied, we turn it round with pleasure and look over it long and well. God's work of creation with man as its summit was so perfected that it brought Him satisfaction. Could he have done more? He did. Through redemption He has brought us through Christ the promise of sharing His rest.

❧

JULY 20

"I . . . fill up on my part that which is lacking of the afflictions of Christ in my flesh for his body's sake, which is the church." Colossians 1:24

The work of Christ as Redeemer is complete, but His afflictions remain to be filled up. Christ has wrought salvation for mankind, yet not all men know what He has done. He Himself only preached the Good News to those of His generation in direct contact with Him. For this reason, we must go and tell the world what Christ has accomplished.

The Apostle Paul is writing of his labors with the gospel among the Gentiles when he speaks of filling up what remains of the afflictions of Christ. Experience had shown him that to the cost paid by Jesus for our redemption there was still a price to be added: the tribulations, distresses, and shame involved in the spreading of the Good News. But this must never deter us from spreading it.

JULY 21

"Wherefore let them also that suffer according to the will of God commit their souls in well-doing unto a faithful Creator."1 Peter 4:19

The creation of man was to meet a need of God: His desire was for communion with a race of men like Himself and for Himself. Redemption, by contrast, is remedial, restoring to God what had been lost by man's rejection of him. Redemption makes possible the recovery and fulfillment of His original and eternal purpose in creation.

We Christians have so stressed God's gift to us in redemption that we have lost sight of His purpose in creation. Redemption is related to us and our well being, that is why we stress it. Creation is related to God and His purpose; that is why it is of such great importance. Thus redemption brings us back to God's beginning, there to be occupied, not just with the satisfying of our needs, but with the fulfilling of God's good pleasure. Should we not be willing to pray and labor and suffer for our faithful Creator?

JULY 22

"Being also joint-heirs of the graces of life." 1 Peter 3:7

God delights in having a husband and wife serve Him together. He blessed the joint ministry of Aquila and Priscilla, as He doubtless did that of Peter and his wife, and Jude and his.

There are three basic reasons for Christian marriage. The first two can be common to all marriages; namely, for the mutual help given and received, and for the institution of family life. The third, however, is peculiar to a Christian couple, for they can receive God's grace together. This clearly shows the importance to God of such marriages. They provide for God a special avenue of bestowal of His grace upon the shared life and upon humanity. Marriage was instituted by God, not by man. Was it for this reason?

JULY 23

"Thy gentleness hath made me great." 2 Samuel 22:36

It frequently happens that God's choice of a leader is quite different from man's ideas of what a leader should be. Even the prophet Samuel had been so influenced by King Saul's stature and strength that when called to anoint a successor, he was ready to believe that Jesse's eldest son matched best the kingly pattern. But neither Eliab nor any of his six brothers was acceptable to God, who all the time looked not at the outward but the inward man. David, He affirmed, was His chosen man.

What did David possess that was lacking in the others? Above all he possessed a heart of dependence on God. It was not a perfect heart. In fact, later in life David had to confess that it was a sinful heart. Nevertheless, it was quite different from that of Saul in this respect, that he displayed a humble willingness to learn. The blessing of God's kingdom is reserved for the poor in spirit.

JULY 24

"I had been intrusted with the gospel of the uncircumcision, even as Peter with the gospel of the circumcision." Galatians 2:7

Paul was a servant of the Lord, but he was different from Peter. No one would suggest that Paul did not preach the gospel. Of course he did. To have done otherwise would have been to repudiate the pioneer work of Peter and throw away the ground gained by him. Do not let us make the mistake of thinking there was some basic conflict between the ministries of these two men, or that the ministries of God's servants should ever be in conflict. Paul makes it clear, in writing to the Galatians, that such differences as there were were related to geography and race, and that in essence their tasks were complementary, not only by mutual consent, but in their value to and attestation by God.

It is very good to read the closing verses of Peter's last epistle, in which he refers to "the wisdom" given to his beloved brother Paul. He may have needed grace to do that. Do we not sometimes need grace to honor one another like that?

JULY 25

"Be not unequally yoked with unbelievers."
2 Corinthians 6:14

Many people seem to think this warning refers exclusively to marriage. I believe that it includes marriage, but that there is far more to it than that. It comprises all kinds of friendship and association between believers and unbelievers. To see this clearly we have only to read the five questions which follow in this and the next verse. They set forth five contrasts that are totally incompatible.

Consider how unequal is that yoke. You are a man of God, but he has no faith. You believe, but he does not believe. You know God, but he has no such knowledge. Whereas you can trust God for every need, he has no one to trust, so must look to himself. You would place everything you possess or plan into God's hands, but he is determined to keep all things in his own hand. Believing God is as natural as breathing to you, but is something totally foreign to him. Tell me: What portion has a believer with an unbeliever?

"Enter into thine inner chamber, and having shut thy door, pray to thy Father who is in secret." Matthew 6:6

Here the phrase "thine inner chamber" is figurative. Just as "synagogues" and "street corners" represent public and exposed places, so "inner chamber" means a hidden place. But let me remind you that you may find a spiritual inner chamber on literal street corners and in literal synagogues. You can pray in secret, that is, on a noisy thoroughfare or in a crowded room. Why? Because an inner chamber is any place at all where you commune with God privately, and any circumstance where you can speak with him without a conscious display of your prayer. "Having shut thy door" means shutting out the world and shutting yourself in with God.

Such prayer is an exercise of faith. It requires that although your senses register nothing, you are praying to a Father who is really attentive, taking account of your prayer. And He is not only observing: He is even going to recompense you. Can you believe this?

"Then shall I know fully even as also I was fully known." 1 Corinthians 13:12

When we come before the judgment seat of Christ we shall stand there, not only to be assessed by God, but that He may explain certain things to us—things which seem all wrong now, but which are His perfect will. In many cases we will have to confess that where we had thought we were right, it is clear now that we were quite wrong. In other cases, however, the Lord will assure us that in fact we were right, but that He was right also.

Not to be offended with the Lord is the highest form of discipline and carries with it a special blessing. There are times when it really seems to us that God is not acting according to His promise. Somehow He seems less than His Word. In fact, He is always better than His Word. We must trust Him now: we shall know it all then.

JULY 28

"Fathers, provoke not your children, that they be not discouraged." Colossians 3:21

There is more instruction in the New Testament for parents than for children. This may be because the occupation of being a parent is harder than any other. It requires a God-given sensitivity. Authority must be used with restraint, because its excessive use may stiffen resistance. This verse warns us that insensitive parents can easily provoke their children to the point of discouragement.

In every way you are stronger than your child. You may subdue him by an overbearing will or simply by your physical strength. If you goad him to such an extent, then he will just wait for the day of liberation. When that day comes, he will throw off all restraint and claim freedom in everything. Ask yourselves, therefore, what kind of home it was that led the needy son to resolve, "I will arise and go to my father."

JULY 29

"God shall wipe away every tear from their eyes."
Revelation 7:17

I delight greatly in the New Jerusalem, not because it has a street of pure gold and twelve gates of pearl, but because there will be the presence of the Lord and the absence of any more tears. We may die and rest in Christ, yet we are not just waiting for death, but for the coming day when the world shall weep no more.

The New Jerusalem is coming very soon, and this tearful world will pass instantly away. On that day the Lord will give us a resurrection body. I think that that body will be similar to the one we have today, possessing all the different members it has now. But it will be a transformed body. And in this transformed body one thing will be missing—tears in the eyes. The Lord has borne our pain so that we may not suffer again in the future. Thank God for the prospect of no more tears forever.

"Is any among you sick? Let him call for the elders of the church; and let them pray over him . . . And if he have committed sins, it shall be forgiven him."
James 5:14, 15

This seems a peculiar kind of forgiveness. Can you find elsewhere in the Bible that if the elders pray for you, you will be forgiven? No, if you sin you must confess to God and you will receive His forgiveness direct. Why does James advise you to call for the elders of the church to pray so that you can know forgiveness?

In the Scriptures it is clear that there is what can be called the government of God, the chief principle of which is that you reap what you have sown. It seems that James writes for the man who may be suffering sickness because of God's governmental hand upon him. No one knows clearly, so he and the elders meet and confess and pray together in the fellowship of the Body. The hand of God is lifted then, and fellowship is restored.

JULY 31

"Put ye on the Lord Jesus Christ." Romans 13:14

When we go to visit people, we always think of our dress. Now in the same way, when anyone thinks of approaching God, he knows he must be clothed with righteousness because without it he cannot meet God. For this reason, righteousness is a fundamental issue in Christian living.

Forgiveness is like taking a bath, whereas righteousness is like wearing a robe. Among men we are clothed so that we may appear before them. So, too, God clothes us with righteousness so that we may live before Him. Does God's Word say that He will clothe us with the righteous robe of the Lord Jesus, or that He will clothe us with the Lord Jesus as our righteous robe? In point of fact, what we do read is that we are to be clothed with the Lord Jesus Himself. We are to put Him on. Thus clad, we can walk before God with boldness at all times.

AUGUST 1

"[God] raised us up . . . to sit with him in the heavenly places, in Christ Jesus." Ephesians 2:6

Redemption is comparable to the valley between two peaks. As one descends from one peak and proceeds to ascend the other, he encounters redemption at the lowest part of the valley. Man has fallen, man has departed from God, and the distance between him and God's eternal purpose, represented by the straight line between the peaks, has become greater and greater. To redeem simply means to prevent man from falling any further and to uplift him.

Because Jesus came into the world and died and rose again, man need plunge no lower. Praise God—redemption has brought us back to God's eternal purpose. What God has not obtained in creation and what man has lost in the fall are completely regained in redemption. The redemption that is in Christ Jesus has restored us to our place in the economy of God.

AUGUST 2

"The place whereon thou standest is holy ground."
Exodus 3:5

The tabernacle of Moses had its proper setting in the wilderness. It was God's dwelling among His pilgrim people, a movable tent, never fixed, never settled. By contrast, the Temple that Solomon built for God in His capital city of Jerusalem was fixed, settled, final. The one is the Church today; the other is the Church in the kingdom of God. Today we only have the earnest, represented by the tabernacle, of the coming age. In the Temple everything was new: a new altar, a new laver, a new table, a new lampstand, a new incense altar. But one thing was not new; namely, the ark of testimony that came to rest there. And everything was enlarged to give greater glory to God; but there is one thing that cannot be enlarged, and that is the ark, the testimony of God's Son. He is "the same yesterday and today, yea and for ever."

I like to think of the floor of the tabernacle, which was desert sand. This is the fitting scene of our pilgrim life before God. It is here that the testimony of Christ is to be borne by us on dusty feet today.

～

AUGUST 3

"And the Holy Spirit descended in a bodily form, as a dove." Luke 3:22

After the Flood, Noah's dove failed to find a resting place, but after Christ's baptism the dove of the Spirit rested and remained on him. Notice—it rests on Him and not on us apart from Him. Our experience of the Spirit comes through Christ, for He is the only One who has fully pleased the Father.

Apart from the Lord Jesus, we should never come up again from the waters of baptism. It is He who carries us safely through the flood and raises us up from the tomb into newness of life. In ourselves we can never please the Father, but we are accepted in Him. And we could never be anointed by the Holy Spirit unless it were by our being found in Christ, the Anointed One. With Christ as our Head, we know the anointing power of the Spirit.

"And my God shall supply every need of yours according to his riches in glory in Christ Jesus." Philippians 4:19

If a man can trust God, let him go out and work for Him; if not, let him stay at home, for he lacks the first qualification for that work. There is an idea prevalent that if a Christian worker has a settled income, he can be more at leisure for the work and consequently will do it better; but as a matter of fact, in spiritual work there is need for an unsettled income, because that necessitates intimate fellowship with God, constant clear revelation of His will, and direct divine support.

God wishes His workers to be cast on Him alone for financial supplies, so that they cannot but walk in close communion with Him and learn to trust Him continually. A settled income does not foster trust in God and fellowship with Him; but utter dependence on Him for the meeting of one's needs certainly does.

AUGUST 5

"The land whereon thou liest, to thee will I give it, and to thy seed." Genesis 28:13

Look what God says to Jacob! It would not surprise us if He had said these words at the end of Jacob's life, but here they are at the very outset! The whole blessing is presented to him, even while he is still his natural, contriving, crafty self. How is this possible?

Surely only because God knew Himself. He had great confidence in what He Himself would make of this man. He knew that Jacob, so committed to Him, could not escape his hands, and sooner or later would become a vessel unto his honor. "I will give it," He said. There was nothing for Jacob to do. How wonderful that God is a God of such confidence! For God's expectation is in Himself, never in us. Oh, that we might learn the invincibility of our God!

AUGUST 6

"Behold, to obey is better than sacrifice, and to hearken than the fat of rams." 1 Samuel 15:22

The greatest of God's demands upon man is not for him to bear the cross, to serve, to make offerings, or to deny himself. The greatest demand is for him to obey.

The sacrifices offered here by Saul were those called in Leviticus sweet-savor offerings. These had nothing to do with sin, for the sin offerings were never described as a sweet-savor offering to the Lord. These were offered to God for His acceptance and satisfaction. Why, then, did Samuel insist that it would have been better to have obeyed rather than to offer them? Because, as the story makes clear, even in a sacrifice there can be an element of self-will, and that can never honor or please God. Obedience alone is absolutely honoring to Him, for obedience makes God's will its only center.

AUGUST 7

"The Son can do nothing of himself, but what he seeth the Father doing." John 5:19

Like our Lord Jesus, we should listen and wait on God before we try to speak or act for Him. Only they who live in God's presence and learn of Him are really qualified to speak for Him. May I say frankly to my fellow servants that the fault today with many of us is that we are either too bold, too strict, or too overbearing. We dare to speak what we have not heard from God. But by what authority do we thus speak? Who grants us this authority? In what are we superior to other brothers and sisters?

Authority belongs to God alone: no one else possesses it. The man who is to exercise the authority that God delegates to him must first live in His presence, commune with Him continually, and study to know His mind. Then, because it is not his own but God's authority that he meditates, others will be enriched, not crushed, by his utterances.

AUGUST 8

*"I thank him that enabled me . . . appointing me to his
service." 1 Timothy 1:12*

Formerly only those of the house of Aaron
were appointed to the service of God. Anyone else who dared to intrude was immediately
cut off from Israel. Today also only people of one
family may be consecrated to His service; but,
thank God, if we believe in Christ we belong to
that family.

One thing is clear: men do not choose to
consecrate themselves to God; it is God who
chooses them to be set apart to Him. Those
who consider themselves as doing God a favor
by forsaking all to serve Him know little of true
consecration. We are chosen for the honor of
serving God: that is what consecration means.
Since we are chosen, it is a sense of glorious
privilege, rather than any awareness of making
a sacrifice, that fills us.

AUGUST 9

"All authority hath been given unto me in heaven and on earth. Go ye therefore . . ." Matthew 28:18, 19

On this huge earth there is at least one group of people who, by their subjection to him, uphold the authority of God. Though the nations rage defiantly against Him, the Church is the one body proclaiming His authority to the principalities and powers in the heavenly places. Not only is she on the earth today to preach the gospel and grow up into Christ; she is also here to manifest the sovereign rule of God.

The Church is the precise opposite of the nations. While they take counsel together against God and against His Anointed, saying, "Let us break their bonds asunder, and cast away their cords from us." The Church with joy declares that she is ready to put herself under His bonds in order to learn obedience. To obey Him is her life. Is it mine?

ح

AUGUST 10

"For the love of Christ constraineth us."
2 Corinthians 5:14

To be "constrained" means to be tightly held, or to be surrounded so that one cannot escape. When someone is moved by love, he will experience such a sensation. Love will bind him.

Love is therefore the basis of consecration. No one can consecrate himself to God without first sensing the compelling love of Christ. It is futile to talk about consecration if this love is unknown to us, but once it is experienced our self-dedication to Him readily follows. The Lord loved us sinners enough to purchase us back to Himself at the supreme cost of His life. When the love that constrains us is such a love, how could our response of committal to Him be less than wholehearted?

AUGUST 11

"But the fruit of the Spirit is . . . self-control."
Galatians 5:22

The end of this list, and thus the summit of a Christian's spiritual walk, is self-control. What commonly is spoken of as the Holy Spirit's government of us does not mean that He directly controls any part of us. That misunderstanding has lured Christians into passivity, or worse, deception, the end of which road is despair. But if we know that the Spirit is to lead man to the place of self-control, we are on the way to progress in spiritual life.

As believers, it is through our renewed will that the Holy Spirit rules. God's object in creation was to have man with a perfectly free volition, and His purpose in redemption is no different. The Christian is not obliged to obey God mechanically; instead his is the privilege of fulfilling God's desires willingly and actively. We are perfectly free to choose or reject the various charges in the New Testament concerning life and godliness. They would mean nothing if God were to annihilate the operation of our own wills. The choice is ours: flesh or Spirit? And the fruit of the Spirit is self-control.

*

AUGUST 12

"Let him deny himself, and take up his cross daily, and follow me." Luke 9:23

We are said in the Bible to be "crucified" with Christ, but never in relation to sin. Liberation from sin and its consequences is for us an accomplished fact. Man is not required to do anything to achieve it, for he cannot. He need only accept by faith as accomplished the finished work of Christ on the cross, in order himself to reap the benefits of that death for him.

What the Bible does say is that we should take up the cross, in the sense of denying self, and that this should be our continual attitude. The Lord Jesus instructs us several times to follow Him in this. The explanation is that God deals with our "sins" and with our "selves" in two very different ways. To conquer sin the believer needs but a moment; to deny self he will require a whole lifetime. Only once, on the cross, did the Lord Jesus bear our sins, whereas throughout His lifetime He denied himself. The same will be true of us, that denial of self is an experience of long association with Him. We follow Him daily.

AUGUST 13

"I wrote unto you with many tears."
2 Corinthians 2:4

We know that the first letter to the Corinthians was written after Paul had heard from the household of Chloe about the serious condition of the church there. In that letter he had reproved them in straight and severe language for their many errors. Now he tells us that the letter was written out of much anguish of heart and with many tears.

One thing is quite certain: if you want your words to strike home to others, you must first be wounded yourself. Unless you have first been cut to the quick, those fine words of yours will have no impact on your hearers. You must suffer first yourself, and deeply, if you are called to say things that must wound in order to heal. How easy it is to point other people to their faults, but how hard it is to do so with tears!

AUGUST 14

"Not that we are sufficient of ourselves, to account anything as from ourselves; but our sufficiency is from God." 2 Corinthians 3:5

God has His work. It is not your work or mine, nor is it the work of this mission or that church group. It is His own work. Paul once expressed a desire to lay hold on that task or role for which he himself had been taken hold of by Christ Jesus. We can conclude that the Lord Jesus has a specific purpose in taking hold of each of us, and it is that purpose and no other which we ourselves want to engage in. He takes charge of us that we in return may actively cooperate with Him in His work.

Nevertheless, it is still true that we cannot of ourselves do a work that is wholly and absolutely His. We participate as His co-workers. On the one hand, we acknowledge that we cannot lift as much as a little finger to accomplish God's purpose; yet on the other hand, we have been given the status of "fellow workers" with Him. It is a paradox that casts us completely upon the sufficiency of the Holy Spirit.

AUGUST 15

"Blessed art thou, Simon Bar-Jonah: for flesh and blood hath not revealed it unto thee, but my Father."
Matthew 16:17

It may seem strange to us that at this point the Lord should identify Peter as the son of Jonah. What relevance had Peter's human father here? It was the Father in heaven who had shown to him who Jesus was. The light he had received so clearly was not a matter of human instruction or insight. In this matter at least, Peter's earthly paternity seems of no concern at all.

The only purpose which Jesus could have had was to single out Peter in a specially individual way. This Simon, Jonah's son and no other, was the one on whom divine illumination had dawned. Such a revelation of Christ to our hearts is always intensely personal. The Church is not a company of people who copy or borrow from one another, but of those who, like Peter, have firsthand experience of the Father in heaven.

AUGUST 16

"For I Jehovah thy God will hold thy right hand, saying unto thee, Fear not." Isaiah 41:13

To know God in the close relationship of "our Father" who supplies our needs is one thing. To know Him as God the Father eternal, the source and originator of everything, is something more. We have to learn that nothing can hinder God and nothing can help Him. He is almighty.

Before He provides us with the gifts of His grace, our hands are empty. After He has done so, they are full and our hearts are filled with praise. But a day comes when God reaches out His hand to take ours in friendship. Then we need an empty hand to put into His. The question is, do we have one? What of the gifts we received from Him? Have we been nursing them to ourselves? Are we too occupied with the spiritual provisions—the "our Father" daily bread—to put them down and have a hand free for Him? Let go the gift and the experience as things in themselves, and hold to God. They can be done without: God Himself is indispensable.

AUGUST 17

"And it was given unto her that she should array herself in fine linen, bright and pure." Revelation 19:8

We have nothing of which we can boast. From outside to inside there is nothing which is entirely pure. The more we know ourselves, the more we realize how filthy we are; our best deeds and our best intentions are mixed with impurity. Without the cleansing of the blood, it is impossible to be white.

The garments here, however, are not only white but bright or shining. Whiteness alone has a tendency to become dull, pale, and ordinary. So it is possible for us to be good and yet to lack divine luster. God's desire for us is that we should be both pure and bright. Now we shall find that tribulation and glory are often linked in Scripture, and it was because of the suffering of death that Jesus was crowned with glory and honor. We must therefore not be afraid of affliction. It is the days of difficulty which make us shine.

❧

AUGUST 18

"For after this manner aforetime the holy women also, who hoped in God, adorned themselves." 1 Peter 3:5

Unless I am mistaken, this is the only place in the Bible where a direct reference is made to "holy women," though the term "holy men" is often used. It is a notable reference because it draws attention to what is of great price in the sight of God. Why should this adornment of a meek and quiet spirit (verse 4) be so valuable in God's eyes? Surely because its loveliness is the beauty of Jesus.

It is unseemly for a woman to be beautifully dressed and yet to display an ugly temper. The apostle would not wish that any Christian woman should be carelessly or negligently dressed, but he rightly stresses that the greatest beauty of all is beauty of character. What is more it wears well, for it is incorruptible.

AUGUST 19

"Behold, thy King cometh unto thee, meek and riding upon on ass." Matthew 21:5

The Lord Jesus charges us to be meek. How meek He was Himself! To show that His kingship is based not on arrogance, but lowliness, He chose to ride upon an ass. During His earthly life He could easily be approached and readily talked to. So should we be. A Christian should not be aloof, but easily accessible in his personal relations.

To be meek in disposition is to be self-controlled. We will not lose our temper. Kindness is the most delicate of human emotions, rudeness and loss of temper the most ill-mannered. The Son of God was never rude. He did not show arrogance, nor seek recognition in high places. He lived humbly on earth, and God's will for us is that we should do the same, following our humble Lord in His pathway of meekness.

AUGUST 20

"Now is the judgment of this world." John 12:31

I n the New Testament when the word kosmos is used for the world, it refers not only to the material universe and its inhabitants but also to worldly affairs, the whole circle of worldly goods, riches, advantages, pleasures, which though hollow and fleeting stir our desires and seduce us from God. Since the day when Adam opened the door for evil to enter God's creation, this world order has shown itself hostile to God.

When Jesus states that the sentence of judgment has been passed upon this world, He does not mean that the material world or its inhabitants are already judged. For them, the judgment is yet to come. What is here judged is that institution, that harmonious world order of which Satan himself is the originator and head. Scripture thus gives depth to our understanding of the world around us. Indeed, unless we appreciate that the unseen powers behind material things are satanic, we may readily be seduced by them.

AUGUST 21

"In labor and travail, in watchings often, in hunger and thirst." 2 Corinthians 11:27

Here speaks a true man of God. The kingdom of God suffers greatly from the neglectful behavior of would be "spiritual" people who busy themselves with prayer and Bible study, attending only to their own spiritual needs. The Lord's people should trust Him to meet their spiritual no less than their physical needs, and devote themselves meanwhile to the tasks which God has given them to fulfill.

Spiritual life is for spiritual work. Its secret lies in the continuous outflow of that life to others. We should be willing to endure even hunger in order to accomplish what God wants us to do, and be satisfied that our spiritual food is simply to do His will. We shall only lack if we are self-occupied. He who is occupied with the Father's business will find himself perpetually satisfied.

AUGUST 22

"There wrestled a man with him until the breaking of the day." Genesis 32:24

It was not Jacob who wrestled, but God who came and wrestled with him, to bring about his utter surrender. The object of wrestling is to force a man down until he is unable to move, so that he yields to the victor. Jacob was stronger than most, but God conquered. When he would not yield, God "touched him." With one touch he did what great strength would not do.

The thigh is the strongest part of the body, a fitting type of our own natural strength. Your strong point and mine may be quite different from Jacob's. Ambition, boasting, self-love each of us has his own, but for each of us that dislocating work is a definite crisis of experience. What happened looked like a defeat for Jacob, but God said he had prevailed. This is what happens when we surrender, beaten, at God's feet.

AUGUST 23

*"Come unto me, all ye that labor and are heavy laden,
and I will give you rest." Matthew 11:28*

How does the Lord Jesus give us rest? He, as it were, sets Himself before us that we may see him, saying, "I am meek." Meekness means flexibility. He who is meek is able to declare that only what God wants him to have will he have. Whether to possess a thing or not to possess it matters not at all, provided the decision is the Lord's. Having it in the will of God, he can thankfully sing hallelujah; yet not having it in the will of God, he can do just the same.

Meekness means that your decisions are subject to change by Him. Is God free to change your mind? You have announced that He loves you, but will you then fret if He does not grant you what you ask for? Can you sing hallelujah anyway? A man is meek when he is willing to turn around if God so wishes. Whatever renewing of the mind God desires of him, he is open to it. Such a man has perfect rest.

꩜

AUGUST 24

"Beloved, let us love one another: for love is of God."
1 John 4:7

The life within the children of God is so rich that it is possible for them to love all their brothers and sisters in Christ. Such love is the spontaneous fruit of God's Holy Spirit. There is no difference between loving one brother and loving them all, for the same love is shown to the one as to the many. He is loved just because he is a brother, they because they are brethren. The number of persons has no bearing here, for the love expressed is "of God." Brotherly love is love of all the brethren.

Let us be careful lest we do things that violate that love. Do not allow your brotherly love to desert you because of wounds received, for this will have sorry consequences. God has put many brothers and sisters in our way, here and now, to be the targets of love. These give us the opportunity to realize in costly, concrete terms our love toward God. Never boast of your love to God; just learn to show love to the brethren.

AUGUST 25

"We know that we have passed out of death into life, because we love the brethren." 1 John 3:14

Many Christians stand up loyally for what is right, yet by the hardness of their attitude they offend against love. They have grown obsessive about righteousness, but deficient in charity. True, as Christians we should never compromise over the righteousness of God, but at the same time we should not strive with others.

Men and women are won by love, not by its opposite. In your contact with people, do not offend them. It is necessary, certainly, for you to obey God and not tone down His commands, but this should not lead you to offend your fellowmen by your attitude or your words. Hard inflexibility should give way in you to meekness and gentleness. That way, many will be attracted to the Lord. Hardness drives people off, but love draws them.

AUGUST 26

"And Samuel said, Though thou wast little in thine own sight, wast thou not made the head of the tribes of Israel?" 1 Samuel 15:17

Saul was only called to the kingdom of Israel because of the people's insistence that they should be given a king. He was tall and impressive, the type of man who could readily be judged acceptable by most of the people. In spite of the doubtful basis of his position, God gave him every facility, prospered him, and blessed him.

But of course Saul had to be tested, and there are few things more testing than God's prospering, especially when it is obvious to all. The one who has been greatly helped by God should be the humblest of men, but sometimes the very reverse is true. This was so in Saul's case. He failed in faith and obedience, but fundamentally his failure was due to conceit. He had been a humble man in adversity, but his prosperity led him into impatience, presumption, and ugly jealousy. May God keep us little in our own sight!

AUGUST 27

"For no prophecy ever came by the will of man: but men spoke from God, being moved by the Holy Spirit."
2 Peter 1:21

Have you noticed how certain words and images are constantly employed by Paul which were not used by Peter or John or Matthew? Have you seen how Luke has structured his Gospel in one way and Mark in another? Have you observed in the one the note of compassion, in the other of immediacy? On each book the writer leaves his own indelible mark; yet each is the Word of God.

Take courage from this. If God wanted to do so, He could use an ass; indeed He did so once, to speak to Balaam. But the ass only spoke when God's Word was in his mouth; and when God moved on, only an ass remained. Thank God He has chosen you to understand His Word, and live it out, and then give it your own unique emphasis when, in weakness and fear and much trembling, you are called to speak it out for Him.

❧

AUGUST 28

"Peace I leave with you; my peace I give unto you."
John 14:27

God preserves in Himself a quite undisturbed peace. It is that peace of God which, Paul tells us, is to garrison our hearts and thoughts. The word "garrison" means that my foe has to fight through the armed guard at the gates before he can reach me. Before I can be touched, the garrison itself has first to be overcome. So I dare to be as peaceful as God, for the peace that is keeping God is keeping me.

Recall that night before Christ's passion. Everything seemed to be going wrong—a friend going out into the night to betray Him, another drawing a sword in anger, people going into hiding in their eagerness to avoid involvement with him. In the midst of it all Jesus said to those who had come to take Him, "I am He," and He said it so peacefully that instead of Him being nervous, it was they who trembled and fell backward. It is no surprise to us, therefore, that Paul describes this peace as beyond understanding.

"Cast thy burden upon Jehovah, and he will sustain thee." Psalm 55:22

Have you ever watched workmen engaged on the construction of a building as they stand at three different levels of the scaffolding and pass bricks from the lowest to mid-level and from there to the top? The work goes on apace as long as each brick, when it reaches one level, is passed on to the level above. What if the man in the middle did not hand on his brick, and yet another came up to him? What if the man at the top level refused to receive the bricks? The poor middle man would be crushed by the load.

That very thing happens to us continually in the unseen. When the first trouble reaches us, we fail to send it on to a higher level, and soon we feel pressed and fretful. Along comes a second trouble, and a third, and by degrees we are worn out and collapse under the load. The remedy is so simple. As soon as any anxiety threatens us, we must immediately pass our burden up higher.

AUGUST 30

"I therefore so run, as not uncertainly."
1 Corinthians 9:26

The Lord who is the Creator of our bodies has endowed them with many legitimate impulses; but remember, He created the body to be our servant and not our master. Until that is established, we cannot serve Him as we ought. Of those who enter the race, Paul warns us, not all are prizewinners. He stresses, therefore, the importance of self-discipline on the part of each competitor.

If in ordinary, everyday life the Christian worker's body has not been taught to know and obey its master, how can it be expected to respond to the extraordinary demands he will sometimes have to make upon it for the sake of the work of God? Paul is no ascetic. He does not teach, as some did, that the body is an encumbrance. On the contrary, he declares that the believer's body is a dwelling-place of the Holy Spirit. Yet as a messenger of the gospel, he is certain of the value of training and self-discipline if the goal is to be attained.

AUGUST 31

"Wherefore leaving the doctrine of the first principles of Christ, let us press on unto perfection." Hebrews 6:1

In the Christian life, there are a few truths which are foundational. A foundation needs to be laid only once, but it must be firmly laid. First principles are therefore very important.

There is a modern error among Christians which is quite different from that of these Hebrews in the first century. They, having laid the foundation, were in danger of circling round and round it, and never going beyond. Our danger, on the other hand, may be that of trying to go forward without ever having laid the good foundation at all. Today some want to move too fast, to rush onward before the foundation has been laid. When that is so, our task is to recall them to Christ, who alone is God's "tried stone, a precious cornerstone of sure foundation" (Isaiah 28:16). The apostles had to persuade people to leave, whereas we may need to induce them to return.

SEPTEMBER 1

"Out of the spoil won in battles did they dedicate to repair the house of Jehovah." 1 Chronicles 26:27

There are Christians whose experiences and whose history with God contribute immensely to the enrichment of His people. Many sicknesses of His children are for the wealth of the Church; many sufferings and difficulties and frustrations bring to it great increase.

There was a sister in Christ who had been bedridden for forty years, during thirty-five of which she had been also cut off by deafness. To a servant of God visiting her she said, "Formerly I was very active, running hither and thither, doing a lot; but I did not help to fulfill the many needs of prayer in the Church. Then that all changed. Throughout these forty years in bed, I have been able daily to engage in the work of prayer. I have no regrets." Distress and limitation had enlarged her and made her rich, and her richness had fed wealth to the Church. How many more there are who are situated like her! We do well to thank God for them.

SEPTEMBER 2

"Jesus saith unto her, Mary. She turneth herself, and saith unto him in Hebrew, Rabboni; which is to say, Teacher." John 20:16

Life can be quite overwhelming when we see no future and are only conscious of bitter sorrow. There are some sorrows that no one else can share. Mary found it so, and stood weeping at the door of the empty tomb. If we feel that we have something to cry about, how much more had she, for she could not find her Lord. In coming to the grave she only expected to find a corpse, but now even that was gone.

What was it that dried her tears and banished all her sorrows? What happened? It was just a voice saying "Mary," but it was His voice and it was her name. After that, nothing seemed to matter. So with us. When we come to an impasse from which there seems no deliverance, we only have to hear the Lord's voice speaking our name, and all is well. There is nothing more to do than to kneel down and worship Him.

SEPTEMBER 3

"Shall we not much rather be in subjection unto the Father of our spirits, and live?" Hebrews 12:9

Do not think that the difficulties you encounter are incidental. Do not ignorantly regard them as mere accidents. You should know better; these things are arranged daily for you by God. They are His measured discipline of love. I once witnessed a scene which may serve as an illustration. I saw five or six children playing in a yard. All of them were covered with mud. A mother came and boxed the ears of three of the children, forbidding them to go on with the game. One child exclaimed, "Why don't you strike the others too?" "Because they are not my own children," she replied.

It will be a sad thing if God does not discipline you. All sons are disciplined, and you should be no exception.

꧁

SEPTEMBER 4

"Ye turned unto God from idols, to serve a living and true God, and to wait for his Son from heaven."
1 Thessalonians 1:9, 10

Many scholars of prophecy do not really know how to wait for the Lord's return. I knew a missionary sister from the West who truly looked for His appearing. I remember how on the last day of 1925, at Pagoda Anchorage, I was praying with her. "O Lord," she prayed, "will You really allow this year to pass away? Must You wait until 1926 to come back? Even on this last day of the year I still ask You to come today." I knew how genuine was her prayer.

Several months later I met her on the road. She took my hand and said, "Brother Nee, is it not strange that He has not yet come?" Her words told me that she was not just an expert in prophetic doctrine, as I was fast becoming, but one who had fellowship with the Lord and was really waiting for his return. She showed herself to be a genuine "scholar of Second Coming prophecy." Her heart longing was for the Lord Himself.

SEPTEMBER 5

"Blessed is the man that walketh not in the counsel of the wicked." Psalm 1:1

God does not want us to be found standing with sinners or sitting with scoffers, and so advises us not to walk in their counsel. Unbelievers have a lot of counsel to give. It is most pitiful, however, for children of God who are faced with problems to seek that counsel. Let me tell you that what they counsel is what you cannot do. I too have many unbelieving acquaintances. I know that such people frequently offer advice without your asking for it. As you listen to them, you know at once that their thoughts are focused on one thing: how to profit oneself.

They do not ask if a thing is right, nor whether it is God's will. They have only one motive, and that is man's personal advantage. At times their advice is not only to seek profit, but to seek it at another's expense. How can the believer walk with the unbeliever in such a way of life?

SEPTEMBER 6

"Through him then let us offer a sacrifice of praise to God continually." Hebrews 13:15

Praise of God is Satan's target. I do not say he does not oppose prayer; for you only have to start praying to God and sure enough, he intervenes. Yet even more does he assault the praises of God's children. He would gladly exert all his strength to prevent God receiving one word of praise, for if prayer is frequently a battle, praise is victory. At the sound of it Satan flees. I discovered this during the first two years of my Christian life, and have not ceased to rejoice in the peace of heart it has brought me.

Let us not, however, make the mistake of equating praise with joyfulness. Look at the Scriptures. It was out of the pressure upon His people that God drew forth so many of the songs that there delight us. He does not measure praise merely by its exuberance. For in its nature praise is sacrifice. Not only must we exalt His name when we stand on the summit and view the promised land; we must learn also to compose psalms of confidence in Him when we walk through the valley of the shadow. This is praise in truth.

SEPTEMBER 7

"I am doing a great work, so that I cannot come down:
why should the work cease, while I leave it?"
Nehemiah 6:3

When the nation of Israel had so sinned that God must give them into captivity, He was already making His own plans to restore them to their land again. Among the instruments whom He prepared for this purpose was Nehemiah, a man whose spirit was in the land of God's promise even while he himself served as a captive exile in the Persian palace of Shushan.

In asking the king for permission to return to Judah, Nehemiah knew he was risking his life. He succeeded in his request, but as he set out on his journey he could hardly have foreseen the opposition he would meet on his arrival there. Yet whatever the enticements, he never once deviated from his "great work" of building for God. Steadfastness of purpose marked him. It is also our secret of spiritual triumph.

SEPTEMBER 8

". . . and the vainglory of life, is not of the Father, but is of the world." 1 John 2:16

John here identifies what stirs pride in us all as the spirit of the world. We know only too well that even in the seclusion of our own homes we are as prone to fall a prey to the pride of life as are those who enjoy great public success. For every glory that is not glory to God is vain glory, and it is amazing what paltry successes can produce in us vainglory. Give way to it, and we have given way to the world, with a consequent leakage in our fellowship with God.

Oh, that God would open our eyes to see how subtle the world is! Not only evil things, but all those things that draw us ever so gently away from Him are forces in that system that is antagonistic to God. If it is the pride of life and not the praise of God which inspires us, then we can know for certain that we have touched the world. Let us therefore watch and pray. Our communion with God is too precious to be put at risk.

"But if a man walk in the night, he stumbleth, because the light is not in him." John 11:10

God is light, and seeing God is seeing light. Seeing light requires a pure heart, a heart adjusted to the love of God. God is as the sun, and I am as a mirror. Unless the mirror faces the sun, it cannot reflect the sun's rays. Should it not be rightly aligned, then the sunlight cannot reach it and so cannot be reflected. The value is lost. Have you noticed that if your heart is deflected from simple devotion to God, then what comes out in your talk will not reflect Him; you will criticize and grumble. This is always proof that you are in the darkness and not in the light.

Some of the Lord's people can continue to praise Him while shedding tears, for although they suffer heartaches they do not stumble. It is because their hearts are inclined toward God that they live in the light. If what you want is man's praise and you do not receive it, then you stumble. If instead your heart only wants His pleasure, then even if circumstances worsen tenfold you still will not stumble.

SEPTEMBER 10

"But go, tell his disciples and Peter, He goeth before you into Galilee: there shall ye see him, as he said unto you." Mark 16:7

". . . and Peter." The tears start to our eyes unbidden when we read these two words. Why does the Lord not single out John, the beloved disciple? Why does lie not make special mention of Thomas the doubter? Why single out Peter from all the others? There is only one answer: because Peter had denied Him.

Suppose you had been Peter, how would you have felt if you had denied the Lord? Might you not have said to yourself, "I, Peter, who was a witness of Jesus' transfiguration; I who was His companion in the garden; I have denied Him. And not just once, but three times over! And to think that the Lord warned me beforehand and I did not believe Him!" Guilty of an offense so grave, Peter might well question his standing before God. For had not Jesus himself solemnly warned his disciples, "Whosoever shall deny me before men, him will I also deny before my Father which is in heaven"? "Tell . . . Peter!" That simple short message showed Peter that

the yawning gulf between him and his Lord had
been spanned by love.

SEPTEMBER 11

*"This is the day which Jehovah hath made; we will
rejoice and be glad in it." Psalm 118:24*

The day which the Lord had appointed was
the day when the stone rejected by the
builders became the chief cornerstone. Who decides whether a stone is usable or not? It is the
builders. If the mason says that a certain stone
is unfit to build the house, you do not need to
ask anybody else. But a strange thing has happened. The stone which the builders rejected
has become the head of the corner. God has put
upon it the most important responsibility. This
is indeed marvelous in our eyes.

The sequel, however, is an added marvel. It is
the appointment of a special day, based on that
divine choice of Jesus Christ as the chief cornerstone. Let us, then, find out what day it was. We
discover it in Acts 4:10 ff. It is the day when He
whom men rejected was raised from the dead.
Let there be no confusion. The Bible puts it very
clearly that this day which the Lord has made is

the day of resurrection. So let all the children of God gather on this day in His Son's name and be glad.

❧

SEPTEMBER 12

"And he that believeth on him shall not be put to shame." 1 Peter 2:6

On His cross the Lord Jesus bore all our shame. The Bible records that the soldiers took the garments of Jesus off Him, so that He was nearly naked when He was crucified. This is one of the shames of the cross. Sin takes our radiant garment away and renders us naked. Our Lord was stripped bare before Pilate and again on Calvary.

How would His holy soul react to such abuse? Would it not insult His sensitive nature and cover Him with shame? Because every man had enjoyed the apparent glory of sin, so the Savior must endure its real indignity. Such was His love for us that He "endured the cross, despising the shame," and since He did so, whoever believes in Him will never be put to shame.

SEPTEMBER 13

"And he fell upon the earth, and heard a voice saying unto him, Saul, Saul, why persecutest thou me?"
Acts 9:4

How can Saul, one earthly creature armed only with a letter from another, be said to "persecute" Jesus of Nazareth who sits at the Father's right hand? The Lord did not say, "Why do you persecute my people?" Instead He asked, "Why do you persecute me?" Christ was certainly in the glory, but the Christ whom Saul persecuted was somehow also on earth.

This is of the greatest significance. Here at once, by implication, Saul of Tarsus is confronted with the Body of Christ—the Head and His members united in one. The oneness of the Body of Christ is not just a future reality in heaven. Were that so, we could only speak of His splendor. But He can be persecuted, so it is also a present fact on earth. Indeed, it links heaven and earth, Head and members, with a unity that God demands shall find a real practical expression down here.

SEPTEMBER 14

"They were thrust out of Egypt, and could not tarry."
Exodus 12:39

All who are saved by grace are redeemed by
the blood. Let us remember, however, that
like the Israelites, once we have been redeemed
we must make our exit. The atoning blood not
only divides the living from the dead; it also
separates God's children from bondage to the
world. The Israelites killed the lamb before mid-
night and after they had put the blood on the
doorposts and the lintel, they hurriedly ate their
meal. They ate it dressed for travel, with their
loins girded, their shoes on their feet, and their
staves in their hands, for they were all set to flee
out of Egypt.

The first effect of redemption is separation. It
does not take several years for this to happen. On
the very night that one is redeemed, he is separated from the world. He is not allowed several
days of deliberation to decide that he will come
out of the world. God never redeems anyone and
leaves him in the world to live on as before. The
saved man takes his staff and moves out. A staff is
for journeying. It is no use as a pillow.

SEPTEMBER 15

"Holding fast the Head, from whom all the body . . . increaseth with the increase of God." Colossians 2:19

Although we are to be diligent in maintaining fellowship in the Body of Christ, we are not told to attach ourselves to our fellow members, but to hold fast the Head. If we are absolutely right with the Lord, then we will be right with fellow believers. There is no possessive relationship between the members; all is through Christ.

If Christ is the Head, then you or I cannot be. The decisions that we make, we make not from personal choice but in obedience to Him; and I cannot decide for you nor you for me. I cannot be your head, for no human body obeys two heads! Alas, it sometimes seems that Christ's Body has too many would-be heads down here. No, let us abandon the ambition to control one another. Christ alone is the Head of us all.

SEPTEMBER 16

"Hold fast that which thou host, that no one take thy crown." Revelation 3:11

In most of the seven churches of Asia it is not difficult to discern what it was that the overcomers needed to conquer. In Philadelphia, however, everything seemed to be acceptable to the Lord. We might feel that this was a church after His own heart, a pattern church, with no reason for a special call to its members to be overcomers. Yet the call was made there too, just as in the other six.

The one hint of warning given by the Lord Jesus was that the Philadelphians should hold fast to their spiritual position. This, then, was the sphere in which they must fight and overcome. Their peril was not so much that of doing what was wrong as of failing to keep on steadily in the pathway of God's will. We all need this same urge from the Lord Jesus, to keep it up right to the moment of His return.

SEPTEMBER 17

"And the law of kindness is on her tongue."
Proverbs 31:26

In joining two people together as husband and wife, God has arranged that there should be subjection and love in the family. He has not asked the husband and wife to find and correct each other's faults. He has not set up husbands to be instructors to their wives, or wives to be teachers to their husbands. A husband need not change his wife or a wife her husband. Whatever the manner of person you marry, you must expect to live with that for life. Married people should learn to know when to close their eyes. They should learn to love and not try to correct.

As Christians, we must learn to deny ourselves. To deny oneself means to accommodate oneself to others. Family life requires discipline. It means learning to be willing to lay aside your own opinion, in giving due consideration to the views of others.

SEPTEMBER 18

"Moses put of the blood upon the tip of their right ear, and upon the thumb of their right hand, and upon the great toe of their right foot." Leviticus 8:24

In the cleansing of the leper and in the conse-cration of the priests, blood was smeared upon the ear, the hand, and the foot, and thereafter oil was put upon the blood-stained parts. Elsewhere in Scripture the blood speaks of redemption, and is only through God. There it is objective. Here, however, it is subjective and betokens the working of death.

The blood on ear, hand, and foot indicates that the Lord's priests must let the cross deal with all they hear and with all their work and their walk, selecting, sifting, and discriminat-ing. The anointing of the Spirit comes where the cross has first been allowed to do its work. When God wants anyone to serve Him, it is not quick-ness of brain or warmth of heart that He looks for. He looks for the marks of the cross on ear and hand and foot.

SEPTEMBER 19

"Mine eyes have seen the King, Jehovah of hosts."
Isaiah 6:5

B efore sending Isaiah forth as His prophet,
God showed Him His glory. Exposed to that
radiance Isaiah could only cry out in dismay,
"Woe is me!" Prior to seeing the Lord, his lips
were already unclean and he had already been
dwelling in the midst of a people of unclean lips;
yet he was unaware of all this. He might easily
have considered himself fit to be a prophet to
God's people—until that light shone down on
him and he saw his actual state and theirs.

How could he now become God's mouth-
piece, since his own lips were so defiled? The one
thing that made it possible was his response in
the face of God's holiness—this cry of "Woe!"
Given such self-knowledge, he was ready for the
seraph to come from the altar and cleanse his
lips. Let us, then, keep the sequence in view, for
it is a good one: first the uncleanness, then God's
light, followed by the cry of self-knowledge, then
the touch of cleansing, and finally the commission to go and serve.

SEPTEMBER 20

"Hallowed be thy name." Matthew 6:9

God's name is linked with His glory. "I had regard for My holy name, which the children of Israel had profaned among the nations," God said through Ezekiel. The people of God had not hallowed His name; they had instead profaned that name wherever they went. Yet God had regard for His holy name, and He calls us to share His desire that it be hallowed.

It is not enough that we should pray the words; we need to have our whole lives governed by this holy desire. Every day will bring its own challenge to us, asking, Is this just a pious fancy, or a governing factor in our lives? The hallowing of God's name must begin in the life of the one who prays the prayer.

SEPTEMBER 21

"Yea, Father, for so it was well-pleasing in thy sight."
Matthew 11:26

"It does not really matter at all," the Lord seemed to be saying, "if the people of Chorazin, Bethsaida, or Capernaum who have received My help do not know Me. Not even the misunderstanding of John the Baptist really matters. One thing only is important, and that is that My Father knows me. If the Father knows, then I am satisfied."

The Father knew Him; but Jesus adds (verse 27) that he alone knew the Father and could reveal the Father to others. This has a parallel in us His servants. Are you willing to be known through and through by God and by Him alone, or do the opinions of those you serve matter more to you? You cannot lead anyone to God if that is what you want. But surely the hostility, the rejection, the misunderstandings matter nothing! It really is sufficient that your Father knows you, and that in return you know Him enough to point others to Him.

SEPTEMBER 22

"He shall . . . bring to your remembrance all that I said unto you." John 14:26

Spiritual words, to ensure their effectiveness, must be kept alive in the Spirit. A certain Christian was once convicted of sin. Others had left the meeting hall where conscience had smitten him, but he remained, overwhelmed, feeling himself under divine judgment. That night he saw sin, in the words of one of our hymns, "as black as smoke." With just those few words he was able thereafter to express vividly the repugnancy of sin in God's eyes. Many were helped and, like him, found forgiveness.

But for two or three years he was harping on the same note. His words, "sin as black as smoke," were still with him; but when he rose to speak, the picture was no longer there. He spoke now, not with tears in his eyes but with a smile. The words were the same, but the man himself was recalling them; the Spirit's reminder was absent. The Holy Spirit had moved on, for the revelation he had given earlier had served its purpose.

❧

SEPTEMBER 23

"While he was wroth with the priests, the leprosy brake forth in his forehead." 2 Chronicles 26:19

How angry we can get when we are not permitted to serve God in the way which we want! King Uzziah was an earnest man who wanted to offer worshipful service to God, but he wanted to do it in his own way. His way, however, was not God's way, and so his anger and his efforts ended in disaster.

"Others can do it," he might have argued, "so why not I? Am I not as good as they are?" Our sphere of service is not to be decided in this way. It is not a question of merit, but of the divine purpose. Uzziah became very heated when he was not allowed to take this service to God into his own hands, but the heat of the flesh was of no avail. His service was rejected, and he never entered the house of God again. We serve God best when we humbly accept His will as He makes it known to us.

SEPTEMBER 24

"Draw me; we will run after thee." Song of Songs 1:4

Our spiritual energy in following Christ springs from more than inward impulse, even by the indwelling Spirit. It results rather from some power drawing us to Him as the Spirit makes Him more real and precious to us through the Word. Far beyond our experience, we are given new revelations of the beauty and majesty of our Lord, and as a consequence are pulled by an irresistible longing to approach ever closer to Him.

Notice the effect that such a devoted following of Christ has upon others. It is I who am drawn, but it is we who run after Him. In other words, there is something contagious and inspiring about a Christ-dominated life. What a privilege to be so drawn by His love that we influence others to run after the Lord in pursuit of their own closer walk with Him!

"Nay but, O man, who art thou that repliest against God? Shall the thing formed say to him that formed it, 'Why didst thou make me thus?'" Romans 9:20

Men always like to reason; but I might well ask if there is any reason why I should have been saved. There is no reason whatsoever. I have neither willed it nor contributed to it, and yet I am saved. This is the most unreasonable thing which has ever happened to me.

When I was young I was frequently offended by the seemingly unreasonable things which God did. Later I read Romans 9, and for the first time in my life I began to see my own littleness and God's greatness. He is so far above all in unapproachable splendor that the glimpse of a tiny fraction of His glory would send us to our knees and make us abandon our reasonings. The Queen of the South was shown a small part of the glory of Solomon, and there was no more spirit left in her. In the presence of Him who is greater than Solomon, what matters my feeble reasoning?

SEPTEMBER 26

"As poor, yet making many rich." 2 Corinthians 6:10

We may be as frugal as we like where our private affairs are concerned, but we must not try to be sparing in the Lord's service, for that will be to deny Him the opportunity of working miracles on behalf of the multitudes. Our attempts at frugality will frustrate His purpose as well as impoverish our own lives.

We come far short as Christian workers if we can only exercise faith for the meeting of our own needs and do not reach out to others in want. We may think as His servants that like the Levites we are entitled to expect God's people to offer us their tenth. What we are prone to forget, however, is that the Levites were in turn under obligation to offer their tenth. Every Christian, no matter how small his assets, should always be a giver. Only to receive, without giving, is to court the disaster of spiritual stagnation.

SEPTEMBER 27

"I can do all things in him that strengtheneth me."
Philippians 4:13

Christ is my health forever. Praise Him, this is a fact. To have the Lord heal me, and to have Him as my healing are two very different things. May I remind you that Paul does not tell us he obtained healing as a thing in itself. What he says is that in his life he continued to have One who was his health. Though his weakness persisted, his healing also persisted. His weakness might be prolonged, but his health was prolonged too.

Most of us think of healing as a matter of elimination, but it is not that at all. It is the life-giving Person of the indwelling Christ. Healing is, for us, not the absence of weakness, but the presence of a vital Power.

SEPTEMBER 28

"Stand therefore, having girded your loins with truth."
Ephesians 6:14

The spiritual warfare is defensive, not offensive, for the Lord Jesus has already fought the battle and won the victory. The work of the Church here on earth is simply to guard and maintain that victory. It is not to overcome the devil, but to resist an already defeated foe. Her work is not to bind the strong man; the strong man has already been bound. Her work is not to let him be loosed.

There is no need to attack; simply to guard is sufficient. The starting point of the spiritual warfare is to stand upon the victory of Christ; it is to keep in view the fact that he has overcome. It is not to deal with Satan, but to trust the Lord. It is not to hope that we will win the victory, because His victory is already ours. Let us gird our loins with this truth.

SEPTEMBER 29

"But of him are ye in Christ Jesus." 1 Corinthians 1:30

Here I must share with you my experience. Back in 1927 I came to the point where I knew that there was a lack of something in my life. Sin was defeating me, and I saw that something was fundamentally wrong. I asked God to show me the meaning of the expression "I have been crucified with Christ." For some months I prayed earnestly and read the Scriptures, seeking light. It became increasingly clear to me that when speaking of this subject God nowhere says, "You must be," but always "You have been." Yet in view of my constant failures, this just did not seem possible.

Then one morning I came in my reading to this verse: "You are in Christ Jesus." I looked again. "That you are in Christ, is God's doing." It was amazing! Then if Christ died, and that is a certain fact, and if God put me into Him, then I must have died too. I have been crucified with Christ! I cannot tell you what a wonderful discovery that was.

SEPTEMBER 30

"And the Word became flesh, and dwelt among us (and we beheld his glory)." John 1:14

There came a time when God committed Himself to human form in the person of Jesus of Nazareth. Before the Word became flesh, God's fullness knew no bounds. However, once the incarnation became a reality, His work and His power on earth were committed to this flesh. Would the Son of man, Christ Jesus, restrict God or manifest Him? We are shown from the Bible that far from limiting God, He has instead wonderfully manifested God's fullness.

Then the time came for Christ to distribute His life to His disciples. There, we may feel, the restriction really began! For nearly 2,000 years God has been working in the Church toward the day when, in the fullest sense, His glory will be no longer restricted. Do we realize this? If we do, will we not spontaneously lift our eyes to him and cry, "O God, how we have hindered Thee! How we have limited Thy power and Thy glory! Find a way through us, even now, freely to manifest Thy glory!"

OCTOBER 1

"He that raised up Christ Jesus from the dead shall give life also to your mortal bodies through his Spirit that dwelleth in you." Romans 8:11

The previous verse explains how God gives life to our spirit; this verse tells us how He gives life to our body. The body is dead in the sense that it is traveling toward the grave. No matter how advanced a Christian's spiritual walk is, he has yet to possess a redeemed body. This can only be in the future. Today's body is just an earthly tent, a body of humiliation.

This verse, however, teaches us that if the Spirit of God abides in us, then through this indwelling power God also gives renewal to that earthly tent. He is not here speaking of a future resurrection, but of the fact that the Holy Spirit can strengthen our physical bodies so that we can meet the requirements of God's work. Neither our life nor the kingdom of God will suffer through the weakness of a body thus renewed and empowered.

OCTOBER 2

"I was dumb, I opened not my mouth; because thou didst it." Psalm 39:9

These words express a fitting attitude for lovers of God. Since He makes all things work together for their good, then this act of His which has befallen me can only be for my benefit. I will yield to it, therefore, without protest, not even asking why my lot differs from the lot of others.

Only if my love is directed, not at God, but at some object I am seeking for its own sake will the good which He wishes to give me be deferred. Lack of an explanation matters little. The way of knowing God is by love and not by knowledge. When I recall how the Lord Jesus said of the sparrows, "Not one of them shall fall on the ground without your Father," should I not accept in silence what comes to me from His hand, seeing the love that has planned it?

~

OCTOBER 3

"He that heareth my word, and believeth him that sent me, hath eternal life." John 5:24

The Epistle to the Romans tells us in much detail about the way of salvation, and from a study of it we can learn a great deal about the doctrine of redemption; and yet it was written for the saved. John's Gospel gives no doctrine in any systematic form; and yet it was written for the world. We would have arranged things the other way round, and we should have been wrong!

If your house is on fire, with you on the top story, and if the firemen come and set up a ladder to save you, will you say, "Not so fast! Tell me first why your ladder does not have to lean on anything. And what materials are your clothes made of that they do not catch fire?" No, you will allow yourself to be saved, and afterward you may inquire all about the fire escape and the firemen's uniforms and anything else that interests you.

OCTOBER 4

"Jesus said unto him, Thou host both seen him, and he it is that speaketh with thee." John 9:37

This man had had his eyes wonderfully opened to see Jesus. Truly to see Him, and not merely to judge Him by outward appearance, is nothing short of a divine miracle. Some in Galilee wrongly took Jesus for Elijah. Now Elijah was a prophet of action who faced opponents with courage and vigor, and the Lord Jesus displayed just such a decisiveness of action. When He found men defiling God's house of prayer with merchandise, He forcibly cast them out. He was a true Elijah.

Others mistook Jesus for Jeremiah. Jeremiah was a figure of divine compassion, a weeping prophet; and Jesus fits in here too. He ate at table with publicans and sinners; He allowed a sinful woman to cry at his feet; and when He saw Mary weeping, He also wept. He was a true Jeremiah. Nevertheless when people mistook Him for either of these, they showed that they knew Him only by appearances. It is the Father's revelation, and that alone, that shows us who the Son really is. Praise God—the man who really saw Jesus could start where we do—"born blind!"

OCTOBER 5

"And while they went away to buy, the bridegroom came." Matthew 25:10

Wherein did the wisdom of the one group and the foolishness of the other lie? Not in the matter of oil, because the lamps of the foolish were still burning, though their oil was low. Their lamps were "going out," that is, not extinguished, but about to be so. Nor was it only a matter of extra oil for replenishing, since the improvident five went off to buy more oil and eventually came back with a sufficient supply.

The difference lay in the fact that the wise had oil in time and the foolish had it too late. It was all a question of readiness and of being in time. It is always wise to be swift in obedience, ready on the spot when called for.

~

OCTOBER 6

*"David said unto Saul, I cannot go with these; for I
have not proved them." 1 Samuel 17:39*

There is no spiritual value conferred by office. Wearing the king's armor does not
give a man kingly qualities. It is striking to remember that David already knew himself to be
the anointed king of Israel. What more natural,
then, than to put on the king's apparel, especially
as he was fighting the king's battles?

He did try the armor, but he soon took it
off again. Inwardly he must have realized that
spiritual power does not come from earthly ac-
companiments, but from a heart relationship
with God. David had entered into such a relationship by secret experiences in daily life. These
hidden victories with God provided him with a
sufficient weapon for his public conflict. He was
much better off without the well-intentioned,
but artificial aids offered by Saul.

OCTOBER 7

"That he might present the church to himself a glorious church, not having spot or wrinkle or any such thing."
Ephesians 5:27

Children and young people have no wrinkles. When wrinkles appear, it means that age is creeping on. But the Lord plans for His Church a condition of unaging life, where there is nothing of decay, nothing of her sorry past. For her He wants everything in its pristine newness. One day, when she stands before Him, it will seem as though she had never had any history of sin. She will be, as God eternally planned, a Church completely Christlike, containing no impurity of man and no savor of sin, having her Lord as her very life.

She will then not only be without spot or wrinkle; she will have no deficiency whatsoever. God will bring the Church to the place where nothing can be said against her in any respect. Mirroring His glory, she will then be completely glorious.

OCTOBER 8

"The time of my departure is come . . . I have finished the course." 2 Timothy 4:6, 7

On at least three occasions Jesus evaded the jaws of death. He did this because He knew that his time had not yet come. The Father had appointed Him an hour, and He knew He should not die in advance of that. The Apostle Paul likewise had the frequent experience of escaping death. He was not afraid to die; nevertheless he clearly trusted in God that he would not die before his work was done.

In the Old Testament we read of patriarchs who died "full of years." This means that they lived out totally the days appointed by God. Whether life be long or short, God intends that we should not perish like sinners before our appointed days are fulfilled. Our years should suffice to accomplish whatever, in His eyes, is our life's work. This is victory over death.

OCTOBER 9

"Let love of the brethren continue." Hebrews 13:1.

God's heart is great and so should ours be. We must learn to have a love large enough to embrace all God's children. If a man is born of the Spirit, then he is a brother. He is a brother if he understands divine truth clearly, and he is still a brother if he does not. If he stays comfortably at home, he is my brother; and if he falls into a ditch on the street, he is my brother still.

Was he baptized by immersion or by sprinkling? Does he believe that the "great tribulation" will last three and a half years, or seven? Is the "rapture" he looks for to be partial or total? If you base your willingness to love him on any such doctrinal questionnaire, you do wrong. Ask only, "Has he the life of Christ or not?" Every one who is redeemed by the precious blood is a brother, and a brother who must be loved.

OCTOBER 10

"Honor all men. Love the brotherhood. Fear God.
Honor the king." 1 Peter 2:17

For the Christian taken up with the joy of fellowship alone with God, the great temptation is to want to do nothing else but remain there basking in His presence. He is in no hurry to return to his former employment with its attendant trials and difficulties. Face to face with the Lord, he senses only joy and holiness and victory; but when he emerges to perform his daily tasks, he encounters discouragement and defeat once more.

Let him be warned that he is in danger of making himself the center, and rendering himself, as a result, unfit to care for the needs of others. Our duty toward men is defined often in Scripture, and our responsibility in the mundane affairs of life is certain. The loftiest Christian experience is never incompatible with the performing of one's duties as a man. To the Lord, there is no conflict between mundane household chores and spiritual ministry. The life of Christ exhibits itself through all sorts of activities.

OCTOBER 11

*"The king hath brought me into his chambers: we will
be glad and rejoice in thee, we will make mention of
thy love more than of wine: rightly do they love thee."*
Song of Songs 1:4

A better rendering of the last clause would
be, "In uprightness they love thee"; that
is, "they love thee without mixture." Paul wrote
to Timothy of "love out of a pure heart and a
good conscience and faith unfeigned," and then
concluded the passage with a reminder that the
Lord Jesus is the eternal King (1 Timothy 1:5,
17). That is the point. The King has brought us
into communion with Himself, and from that
fact there springs a new and satisfying love.

There is a sense in which we can only come
to recognize Christ as the beloved Bridegroom
of our souls if we first yield Him homage as our
King. The justified sinner rightly loves his gracious Savior. Later on, as he grows closer to Him,
he finds that what gives unmixed quality to his
devotion and love is his complete dedication
to the rule of Jesus as his sovereign Lord. He is
learning to love "in uprightness."

OCTOBER 12

"Thou mindest not the things of God, but the things of men." Matthew 16:23

Jesus had scarcely told His disciples of His approaching rendezvous with the cross than Peter burst in, out of his intense love for Him, with the cry, "Lord, pity yourself." The Lord's answer could only be a stern rebuke. Self-pity, Jesus declared, was an idea that could have come only from Satan. He then countered Peter's protest by going further. "It is not I alone who must go to the cross," He told them, "but all of you who follow me and desire to be My disciples. Do not imagine that I am the only one who must do God's will. My way shall be your way too."

Deep down, Peter knew this, and if in saying "Pity yourself" he was expressing affection for the Lord, he was at the same time unconsciously revealing his attitude toward himself. He too would avoid the cross and thus preserve the selfish life of his own soul.

OCTOBER 13

*"But we will continue stedfastly in prayer, and in the
ministry of the word." Acts 6:4*

All ministry, all service to mankind, which
has lost its priestly emphasis has broken
down. If I have not first of all gone into the presence of God, I cannot come forth to my fellows
with any message or service of value to them.

If there is a prophet's ministry without at the
same time a priestly ministry, then there will be
no building of the Church. If my right hand is
injured and in pain, and my left hand wants to
come to its aid, it does not act unbidden. Communication is by way of the head, and action
is initiated there and controlled from there. An
unattached left hand could be no help at all. And
serving our brothers is like that. If we would
avoid causing only trouble with other members,
we should act under direction of the Head; we
should come to them in service straight from the
presence of God.

OCTOBER 14

"What wilt thou that I should do unto thee? And he said, Lord, that I may receive my sight." Luke 18:41

We must guard against belaboring God with words which are not real prayers. Satan delights, not only in depriving us of the time to pray, but also in making us waste the time we have in multiplying scattered, empty words. Many long, wearisome, routine prayers are merely wasting time. If you do not even know what you want when you kneel to pray, how can you expect God to answer? You fall into the trap of thinking you have spent a useful time in prayer when in fact you have not prayed at all.

The Lord will ask you, as he asked blind Bartimaeus, "What do you want Me to do for you?" Can you answer that question specifically and clearly? You should train yourself to do so. We are warned to watch in prayer. Do not drag out the time; do not offer God your many reasons; simply and in plain terms pour out your desire before Him.

OCTOBER 15

"By faith Abraham, when he was called, obeyed to go out." Hebrews 11:8

It is from God, the source and beginning of all things, that His new creation springs. We might fittingly borrow the words of the Lord Jesus who said, "My Father worketh hitherto, and I work." This is a lesson we all have to learn: that we can originate nothing of divine value. God alone is the One who begins everything. Though this fact injures our pride, yet the day we really see it is a day of happiness for us. It seems we have recognized that where eternal values are concerned, all must be from God.

Abraham needed to make no new beginning of his own. God took the initiative with him. And Abraham never thought of Canaan as his goal. He went out ignorant of where he was bound. That was known to God, and he simply responded to a call of God. Blessed is the man who doesn't know! When we really understand that God is the beginning and the end of all that matters in life, we can be at rest.

OCTOBER 16

*"For he was a good man, and full of the Holy Spirit
and of faith." Acts 11:24*

We see people who appear richly endowed
with gifts by God, and we think how
wealthy they are and how greatly He uses them.
Yet what really brings help to those in need is not
these impressive gifts and utterances; it is the life
that rises triumphant over death in those who,
like Paul, "die daily."

God sovereignly bestows gifts upon one here
and one there that they may serve as His mouth-
pieces, but what He really seeks are not spokes-
men but vessels for the communication of that
life by the Spirit. This resurrection life of Jesus
flows out from those in whom "the dying of Jesus" is at work within (2 Corinthians 4:10). He
who puts his trust in spiritual gifts is being foolish, for such gifts do not necessarily work that
transformation in the inner man. It is out of bro-
kenness that there can come forth life.

OCTOBER 17

"I can of myself do nothing." John 5:30

At his creation Adam became a distinct self-conscious person, but he had no sin. There was not yet ruling in him what Paul in Romans 6:6 calls "our old man." He possessed free will, which made it possible for him to act on his own account; so that self, we may say, was already there—but not sin. But then the fall changed all that. Now there was the "old man" dominant in him, and certainly in all of us.

We must be cautious about drawing parallels between ourselves and the Lord Jesus in His incarnation, but we can say with assurance that He had no old man, because He was free from sin. Nevertheless, He had a self. He possessed natural strength; yet not once in the smallest degree did He abuse it. It is not that He lacked an individual personality—every man has that—but that He did not choose to live by Himself. In our verse He makes clear His estimate of the worthlessness of natural human effort apart from God. We can understand, therefore, why He went on to say of our spiritual fruitfulness, "Apart from Me ye can do nothing."

OCTOBER 18

*"In returning and rest shall ye be saved; in quietness
and in confidence shall be your strength." Isaiah 30:15*

Desire for haste bespeaks an emotional nature. Emotion is usually hasty. It is extremely hard for the hasty Christian to wait on
the Lord, to know His will and knowing it, to
walk a step at a time in that will. Indeed we who
are His own are incapable of following the Spirit
until our emotions are truly yielded to the cross.
We need first to learn there the "patience of Jesus
Christ," for let us remember that out of a hundred impatient actions, scarcely one is in the will
of God.

Because He knows the impetuosity of our
nature, God frequently uses our fellow workers,
brethren, family, or environment to put the brake
on us. For God never performs anything hurriedly; consequently, He will rarely entrust His power
to the impatient.

OCTOBER 19

"Whosoever would become great among you shall be your servant [margin]." Matthew 20:26

We who would be leaders must learn not to lord it over those entrusted to our care nor to lead them on faster than their ability to follow. If we have a word from the Lord for them, we should be faithful in sharing it; but we dare not insist that they accept its message. Let us remember that God approves the free will He has given to man; and if He never coerces man, how dare we? Let us learn to walk softly before Him and to be very slow to put ourselves up before men in the role of leader.

It should be no matter for self-gratification that people are ready to learn what we have to say. Rather should it drive us to the Lord in fear and trembling. No matter how strong our convictions, we must learn to distrust ourselves, for we are prone to err; and the more self-assured we are, the more we are liable to go astray. The danger is that the greater the following we attract, the more our self-confidence is fed and the less we are able to receive help from others.

OCTOBER 20

"Upon the first day of the week let each one of you lay by him in store, as he may prosper."
1 Corinthians 16:2

The first day of the week spoken of here is different from the Sabbath of the Old Testament. It is not a day of assessment, nor is it merely a day for physical rest. It directs us rather to two things we especially ought to do. One is to come together to the Lord God in order to receive grace from Him, and the other is to offer to Him our gifts. It is a day for us to rejoice in the Lord.

Is it not surprising to find that our gifts are to be made weekly and not monthly? Many wait until the end of the month, and some may even wait until the year's end, to give their gifts to God, but Paul tells us we must balance our accounts before Him on the first day of each week. Let us note too that each one is free to decide on his own percentage. Give more if you can give more, less if you have less. The important thing is that you should give your portion joyfully.

OCTOBER 21

"But one thing is needful: for Mary hath chosen the good part, which shall not be taken away from her."
Luke 10:42

Jesus never implied that Martha should not work. Indeed, the Bible elsewhere tells us that the man who does not work should not eat. Nor did He propose to Martha that she should spend half her time serving and the other half dealing with matters of the spirit. He never suggested that doing her "many things" was wrong, but He reminded her that she should not let them fret and irritate her. Martha did not engage in too many tasks; she indulged in too many worries.

Thank God that there was also a Mary. She had chosen the best portion, which is communion with the Lord, and she represents the other half of the picture. What Jesus wanted was that Martha should follow her sister's example of peace of heart, even while she worked. We can all be like Martha, occupied with outward things; but at one and the same time we must be like Mary, in fellowship with Christ within. Any man or woman may be outwardly busy while inwardly sitting at the feet of Jesus. That is true service.

OCTOBER 22

"He that loveth not his brother whom he hath seen, cannot love God whom he hath not seen." 1 John 4:20

We might perhaps add to the Apostle John's words, "If we cannot love our brothers whom we see, how can we love the brothers whom we cannot see?" Paul wrote to the Corinthians about love, because love unites. In Corinth there was envy and strife; so Paul told them that love envies not, seeks not her own, thinks no evil of others; in other words, love does not divide and separate. All this was an exhortation to the believers in Corinth to love one another at close quarters.

Many of us are good at brotherly love so long as the brethren concerned are faraway and unseen. It is loving those whom we see everyday that really tests our love for God. The Corinthians were to love their brothers in Corinth first of all. Later, perhaps, they might go to Ephesus and love the members of Christ there. Only later still would they ascend into heaven to see the Body of Christ in its wholeness. This is the right order and the most difficult, for it tests our sincerity.

~

OCTOBER 23

"The fear of man bringeth a snare." Proverbs 29:25

Once there were two men who worked in the same firm. One of them found Christ as his Savior; but it happened that both men were extremely timid. The one who was saved dared not tell the other that this had happened, while the other could not work up enough courage to ask the converted man what had occurred, though he could see the change.

They shared the same table at work. Daily they faced each other, yet one dared not tell and the other dared not ask. At last the one who had believed could stand it no longer; so after much prayer, he went to his friend and said, "I am a most timid man. For at least three months I have not dared to tell you that I have believed in the Lord Jesus." Then his friend answered, "All these three months I have been longing to ask you what has happened." If you live in fear of others, it may help you to remember that perhaps others fear you. Take courage and speak.

OCTOBER 24

"For the kingdom of God is not eating and drinking, but righteousness and peace and joy in the Holy Spirit." Romans 14:17

The Bible allows us great latitude in external things such as food. Why is it that you may eat or not eat as you like? Because from God's viewpoint this is only a minor matter. God attaches no great importance to prohibitions. Instead, He lays stress on what is positive. The life of the Son of God on earth, and Christ's risen life in us—these are the essentials. Having that glory among us, such matters as food and clothing become very minor indeed. That is why the Christian life, as set forth in the Bible, is never legalistic, but wonderfully flexible.

It you wish to dress more moderately and eat less costly food, it is good. But if you have more money and feel like eating better or spending more on clothes, you may do it. The pivotal question is how much spiritual reality is manifested in your life. Do remember that a Christian is not an ascetic. He lives an adaptable life, sensitive always to Him who in us is exceedingly great and glorious, and who is ruled not so much by abstinence as by transcendence.

OCTOBER 25

"A new spirit will I put within you … And I will put my Spirit within you." Ezekiel 36:26, 27

Note here how after the promise of "a new spirit" there immediately follows the allusion to "my Spirit." The first statement signifies the renewal of the dead spirit by an incoming of life in one who believes. The second goes further and points to the indwelling Holy Spirit of God resident within the man's renewed spirit.

But the two are one experience. Christians do not live for many years after new birth in a first phase of Christian life and then suddenly wake up and, seeking the Holy Spirit, enter on a second phase. They have His entire personality abiding in them—not just visiting them—the moment they are saved.

The apostle exhorted us not to grieve the Holy Spirit. By using the word "grieve" and not "anger," he reveals the Holy Spirit's love. Moreover, he certainly never says, "Do not cause Him to depart." It may be the plight of the Spirit to be either grieved or gladdened, but He abides within us forever. There is no question of his leaving.

"Christ also loved the church, and gave himself up for it." Ephesians 5:25

The theme of this verse is not so much the coming of Christ to die for sinners as the giving of Himself to them in love. John tells us how at the cross the soldiers came to examine Jesus. They found to their surprise that He was already dead, but they pierced His side and there flowed out blood and water. This suggests symbolically the two aspects of the work of Christ; namely, the shedding of blood to redeem us from our sins, and the flowing out to us of the water of life.

To die for sins is one thing, but to die for love is more. Christ died for us in order to give himself to us. The vital issue of our new birth lies just here. It is not repentance which makes us a part of Christ, neither is it confession of our sins, nor even our faith. It is the life of Christ imparted to us by a divine act, which alone makes us a part of the Church which He loved and gave Himself up for.

OCTOBER 27

"I counsel thee to buy of me gold refined by fire, that thou mayest become rich." Revelation 3:18

If we desire to continue on the course of Philadelphia and not slip back into that of Laodicea, then we must learn to be humble before God. Sometimes I have heard brothers say, "The blessing of God is in our midst." I acknowledge the truth of this, yet I feel we need to exercise extreme caution in saying it. If one day we incline to say that we are rich and have gotten riches and have need of nothing, we are very close to the condition of Laodicea.

Remember—there is nothing we possess which we did not first receive from God. He who stands before the Lord is not conscious of his own wealth, but only of him. He who comes forth from the Lord's presence is rich, yet he is not aware of his riches. The radiance on Moses' countenance faded, and for him it was better so, for once it became known to him he might have ended up in lukewarmness.

OCTOBER 28

"Did not God choose them that are poor as to the world to be rich in faith?" James 2:5

The goal and reward of temporal poverty is eternal enrichment. God never intended that tribulation and poverty should have no fruit. His purpose is that all pressure should lead to enlargement and that all poverty should lead to wealth. His destiny for His people is not continuous distress nor continuous poverty. Straitness and poverty are not an end; they are the means to an end.

There is much that we do not understand in John's revelation of the New Jerusalem, but we do see there a city of infinite wealth. There is, however, not a nugget of gold in that city which has not been tried in a furnace of affliction, not a precious stone which has not passed through the fires, and not a pearl that has not been born of suffering. To be "rich in faith" is surely justified, therefore.

OCTOBER 29

"Adding on your part all diligence, in your faith supply virtue." 2 Peter 1:5

Peter is telling us here that a continual "adding" should characterize every Christian. We should cultivate a disposition which never ceases to explore fresh territory in the realm of divine things. Although Peter is an old man when he writes this, divine energy pulsates in him and is communicated to his readers.

He urges us that as soon as we have possessed one Christian virtue, we should seek to supplement it with another; and having acquired that, we should heap on yet more. Diligence, faith, virtue, knowledge, self-control, patience, godliness, brotherly love, divine love: Peter's list is long and is summarized by his key word, "abundance." Press on and on, he says, never resting content with your present attainment, never ceasing from this holy task of adding, until the goal of God's purpose for you is reached.

❦

OCTOBER 30

"And he went out, and wept bitterly." Matthew 26:75

In affirming that he would never be offended in Christ, Peter was contradicting his Lord; yet his doing so was no mere bravado. He was confident that he spoke the truth. It was because Peter so firmly believed in himself that Jesus reinforced his general statement regarding all His disciples by adding details of the depth to which Peter would fall in desertion of Him.

Yet so deep-rooted was Peter's self-confidence that all the Lord's assertions failed to convince him. More vehemently than ever he promised his loyalty. He meant every word. He loved Jesus and wanted to follow him unreservedly; and when he spoke as he did, he was expressing the intention of his heart. But he mistook himself for the man he desired to be. Thank God that Peter was brought through breakdown to discover his own weakness. If there was sincerity in his self-confidence, there was sincerity too in his weeping. From that hour of his self-discovery, God was able to fashion him anew.

OCTOBER 31

"Every scripture inspired of God is also profitable . . . that the man of God may be complete." 2 Timothy 3:16, 17

From beginning to end the Bible maintains an organic unity. It is no disorderly compilation of human minds, but is bound together by the working of the Spirit of God, so that what we have today is fully at one with its origins. The five books of Moses stand at the beginning of the record—and this is the significant point: all who wrote afterward built upon them; they did not write independently. Joshua builds on the foundation of the Pentateuch, and so does the author of the books of Samuel.

Though the writers are various, every book in the Old Testament builds on what went before. And when we reach the New Testament the same is true: the New uses the Old as its springboard. You cannot discard the Old Testament and retain only the New Testament; neither can you cut out the four Gospels and keep only the letters of Paul. God does not say one thing yesterday and another thing today. His Word is one. From start to finish, it lives and speaks to our need.

NOVEMBER 1

"For I know nothing against myself; yet am I not hereby justified." 1 Corinthians 4:4

W ho can discern his errors?" asks the psalmist. The answer is, no one. By ourselves we cannot accurately know our faults. If, as Jeremiah said so forcefully, our hearts are deceitful above all things, then how can our attempts at introspection be trustworthy? Examining ourselves with a deceitful heart, we will inevitably be deceived. Our thoughts and emotions are highly complex in their working, so the knowledge derived from them is undependable. We cannot be accurate in our self-judgments.

For this reason, introspection is not a virtue, but a huge mistake. Only when the light of the Lord shines in is one able to discern what is right and what is wrong. If a Christian considers his defects overmuch, he is downcast; if he thinks upon his virtues, he grows proud. The only knowledge of self which is safe and healthy comes from the shining in of the light of God.

NOVEMBER 2

"Suddenly there shone round about him a light out of heaven: and he fell upon the earth." Acts 9:3, 4

Real light from heaven is more than knowledge. It is the discovery of the Lord Himself. Whoever sees Him, sees light; and if we really see light, we will fall to the ground. Instruction does not have this effect. We may listen to any number of instructive sermons and even memorize their content, and still remain unchanged. But that never happens when true light comes from God. When that light dawns, it blinds our eyes to one whole world that they may be opened to another. It does indeed cause us to see, but first it blinds and prostrates us. When Paul saw the light, he was smitten to the ground and for three days could see nothing.

Light is rigorous. It can do to a man what he himself can never do. Like Paul, who truly thought he ought to oppose Jesus, we may be rigid and inflexible, resistant to all persuasion; but when that light shines we are softened, weakened, broken. Light has to humble us before it enables us to see.

NOVEMBER 3

"And he put the whole upon the hands of Aaron, and upon the hands of his sons, and waved them for a wave offering before Jehovah." Leviticus 8:27

In this sacrificial ritual, the blood so placed on Aaron and his sons was taken from "the ram of consecration." When this had been done, then into Aaron's hands was placed "the wave offering." Aaron's action in lifting up this offering to God is what was then called "consecration." Can we now put this in New Testament terms?

According to the acceptance which Christ has before God, I now stand in the position of a servant who hears God's voice, does His will, and walks in His path. Hereafter my ears, my hands, and my feet belong exclusively to God. No one can borrow my ears to listen to another's voice, or my hands to do another's bidding, or my feet to walk in another's path. I even take a further step. I fill my two hands with Christ and uplift him. This means that I am here for the service of God and my whole body is devoted to that service.

NOVEMBER 4

"He that hath seen me hath seen the Father."
John 14:9

The great message of the Bible is that the Word became flesh. There was a time when we did not know what grace and truth were. But today grace is no longer an abstraction, for in the life of the Lord Jesus we have seen how grace lives and walks among men. It has, as it were, become flesh. Similarly, we did not know truth or holiness or patience until we saw them in the Lord Jesus.

God is love, yet we were ignorant of how he loves. Now we have beheld this love come down to us in Jesus of Nazareth. We misunderstood spiritually, thinking that a spiritual man should neither smile nor weep, but be totally devoid of any human feelings. How wrong we were! For in the smiles and tears of the Lord we comprehend what spiritually in fact is. In God, these things were too far off for us to apprehend them. In Jesus, they are close at hand.

NOVEMBER 5

"For this, moreover, will I be inquired of by the house of Israel, to do it for them." Ezekiel 36:37

God is here expressing His purpose to increase the house of Israel like a flock. Those unacquainted with Him will ask why, if He wants to do this, He does not Himself simply give the increase. Surely no one could stand in His way!

But here He states His condition. He will do it for them if He is inquired of concerning it by the house of Israel. The principle is unmistakable: God has a purpose already determined, but He will not force it through unasked.

From this we can move to the Church's function before God today. Never let us think of the Church simply as a place for meetings. No, the Church is a group of people, redeemed by the precious blood, regenerated by the Spirit, and committed into God's hand for the role of inquiry of Him in prayer until His will in the earth is brought to pass. The smallest group of Christians praying contributes to that. God will do whatever He has set Himself to do, through the Church's prayer.

NOVEMBER 6

"But when it was the good pleasure of God, who separated me, even from my mother's womb, and called me through his grace, to reveal his Son in me. . . ."
Galatians 1:15, 16

God had set Paul apart before he was born. Even the profession he learned before his conversion was preplanned. God works like that. All that happened to you before you were saved, as well as after, has some definite meaning. Whatever your character and temperament, whatever your strengths and weaknesses, all are pre-known by God and prepared by Him with future service in view. There is no accident, for everything is within God's providence. Nothing comes by chance.

Having been thus set apart from birth, none of us can afford to be casual or frivolous in our attitude to life. Each one of us must expect to discover what God has planned for us, and in His time and way to enter into it. God does not write off as valueless our unregenerate days. He does not want us to deny the very human elements in our makeup by presenting instead a false, because unreal, front. He has a use for the persons we are and intends to use the real us, purified by the cross, and not some pretense, in his service.

❧

NOVEMBER 7

"And David danced before Jehovah with all his might; and David was girded with a linen ephod."
2 Samuel 6:14

Michal, the daughter of Saul, saw her husband dancing before the ark of God and despised him in her heart. He ought, she believed, to maintain his dignity as king, just as her own father had tried to do. But David viewed things differently. In the presence of God he saw himself as base and contemptible, having no special standing whatever. Though on the throne he was Israel's king, before the ark of God he was on the same level as his subjects.

Even after God had rejected him, King Saul had sought to save his face by asking Samuel the prophet to honor him before the nation. Now Michal was making the same mistake. Born in the palace herself, she considered that David merited the dignity of king in God's presence. Perhaps, like her father, she too had her own majesty to think of. That way lies fruitlessness. The one who wields true authority is otherwise. He will not be high-minded, grasping to preserve his position, but meek and humble before God, a model to his people.

NOVEMBER 8

"And whatsoever ye shall ask in my name, that will I do, that the Father may be glorified in the Son."
John 14:13

We find in John chapters 14, 15, and 16 that the Lord constantly uses the phrase "in My name." Not only does this indicate to us that He will receive from the Father a name above all names. It tells us also that His name is something which His disciples may use. The name of Jesus is what He has received from God: "in the name of Jesus" is what the children of God share. He has trusted us with something of tremendous value. Do we recognize it as the greatest trust which He could have committed to us?

Sometimes we say to a friend, "Go and tell so and so to do this or that," adding, "If he questions it, tell him I say so." This is what is implied by "in my name." It simply means using the name with the power behind it. You give your name with its authority to a certain person; and you are then responsible for whatever he does using your name. The name of the Lord Jesus is unique, a name above all names, nevertheless, He is willing to entrust His name to us, and Himself to take responsibility for our use of it. Do we truly appreciate the honor He does us?

NOVEMBER 9

"And I also say unto thee, that thou art Peter, and upon this rock I will build my church."
Matthew 16:18

Remember that shortly after this the Lord had to say to Simon Peter, "Get behind me, Satan." How could a man overcome by Satan be used to build up a Church against which the gates of Hades were to prove ineffective? We know he could not. Although Simon had received the name Petros, "a rock," his character did not correspond to his name; so as yet he was unable to use the keys of the kingdom.

No one who is of an irresolute temperament can exercise a ministry of opening the doors to welcome men into life. There must be a correspondence between the character of the minister and the confident, even defiant, truth he ministers; namely, that Jesus has died and risen again victorious over death. For Peter, that still lay ahead. But alas, death's gates do prevail over much Christian work, because His servants lack that confidence! Praise God—the cross of Christ released resources enough to transform Peter and to deliver from death all who place their trust in Christ.

NOVEMBER 10

"Arise, get thee to Zarephath; . . . behold, I have commanded a widow woman there to sustain thee."
1 Kings 17:9

Because of our proneness to look at the bucket and forget the fountain, God has frequently to change His means of supply to keep our eyes fixed on the source. So the heavens that before sent us welcome showers become as brass, the streams that refreshed us are allowed to dry up, and the ravens that brought our daily food visit us no longer. But then God surprises us by meeting our needs through a poor widow woman, and so we prove the marvelous resources of God.

We are the representatives of God in this world, and we are here to prove His faithfulness. Our attitudes, our words, and our actions must all declare that He alone is our source of supply, or He will be robbed of the glory that is His due. He who sees in secret will take note of our needs, and He will meet them, not in stinted measure, but "according to His riches in glory by Christ Jesus."

NOVEMBER 11

*"And behold, I am with thee; . . . I will not leave thee,
until I have done that which I have spoken to thee of."*
Genesis 28:15

God is an acting God. We may think that hearing sound doctrine is the only means of grace; but His means are practical, the chastening of experience, the provision of a host of different circumstances in our lives for training and profit. We may, like Jacob, represent unpromising material for Him, but He works on patiently with us. He is more tenacious than we are in the pursuit of His goal.

And here is further ground for encouragement. We do not have to know what work is needed or how it is to be realized in order that God may effect what He has set out to do with us. The most unpromising people of all are those who are wrong but who do not know it; yet even so God has His own way of bringing light into their darkness. In His own time and His own way He will finish the task He has set Himself.

NOVEMBER 12

"Each man's work shall be made manifest: for the day shall declare it." 1 Corinthians 3:13

If wood and hay are unsuitable building materials, how much more so is stubble. It seems to represent what is least reliable of all in the unsubstantial realm of man's efforts. Whenever we build for God according to our feelings, according to the whim of the moment or the applause of the crowd, we are building with stubble. The day will declare it.

Labors that are governed, not by God's program, but by our own fickle emotions, may seem to make such progress at times, but may just as easily fade out. It is so possible to reflect the changing moods of the weather, depending on the wind of revival to arouse an emotional effort that is here today and gone tomorrow. God has made provision in Christ for better, more solid construction than that, as the day will ultimately declare.

NOVEMBER 13

"He was manifested to take away sins; and in him is
no sin. Whosoever abideth in him sinneth not."
1 John 3:5, 6

Some of us force ourselves to do things we don't want to do and to live a life we cannot in fact live, and think that in making this effort we are being Christians. That is very far removed from what God offers us in Christ. The Christian life is lived when I receive the life of Christ within me as a gift, to live by that life.

It is the nature of the life of Christ not to love the world, but to be distinct from it, and to value prayer and the Word and communion with God. These are not things I do naturally; by nature I have to force myself to do them. But God has provided another nature, and He wants me to benefit from the provision He has made. God sets up a standard, but Christ shows us His storehouse. Strength, life, grace from God, all are ours to receive that we may measure up to the divine standard.

NOVEMBER 14

"And Jacob said when he saw them, This is God's host;
and he called the name of that place Mahanaim."
Genesis 32:2

This glimpse of the angels of God should have sufficed to reassure Jacob on his return to Canaan. The verses which follow, however, tell how fear of his brother overcame him and led him to divide his people and possessions into "two companies." Here we find in Hebrew the same word Mahanaim, two hosts, that Jacob had used before. Now, though, he had substituted his own mahanaim for God's. Where there had been "two hosts" before—namely one heavenly company and one earthly, his own—he now forgot the former and divided his earthly company into two. He then prayed his first real prayer.

In Jacob's early years it was all scheming and bargaining, and no prayer. Now it was both scheming and prayer. Yet if we pray, we need not scheme. If we scheme, there is no meaning in our prayer. Jacob, however, did both: on the one hand he trusted God, and on the other hand he did the work himself. Happily for him, it was on that night that God met him.

NOVEMBER 15

"Even so let your light shine before men; that they may see your good works, and glorify your Father who is in heaven." Matthew 5:16

The divine life planted in us, itself so utterly alien to the world around it, is a light-source designed by God to illuminate the world's true character. It does this by emphasizing through contrast the world's inherent darkness. From this it is clear that to separate ourselves from the world today, and thus deprive it of its own light, is no way to glorify God. It merely thwarts His intention of serving mankind through us.

The Church, to use another metaphor, is a thorn in the side of God's adversary, a source of constant annoyance to him. We make a heap of trouble for Satan simply by being in the world. So why leave it? The Church glorifies God, not by getting out of the world, but by radiating His light in it. Heaven is not the place to glorify God; it will be the place to praise Him. The place to glorify Him is here.

NOVEMBER 16

"I have set before thee a door opened, which none can shut." Revelation 3:8

If God is going to have a witness in the earth today, He must have the service of all His less-gifted servants, His "one-talent" men. We might imagine that if He were gracious to His Church, He would give us more people like Paul and Peter; but in fact He seldom does so. The Church of God is full of ordinary, one-talented believers, and if only we would abandon our personal ambitions and seek instead ways for them to serve him, wonderful things would happen.

The Church needs leaders, but it also needs brothers. I believe in authority, but I believe also in brotherly love. In Philadelphia they respected authority, for they kept the Lord's word and did not deny His name. But *philadelphia* in Greek means "brotherly kindness." It was to these caring brothers and sisters that the door was opened. Let them set out to serve Him together and not wait for the specialists; then we shall begin to see what the Church's service really is.

NOVEMBER 17

"Ye are my witnesses. Is there a God besides me? yea, there is no Rock; I know not any." Isaiah 44:8

To witness is not to disseminate knowledge which everyone already has, but to point to truth that few are aware of. Because of conditions generally in the ancient world, God wanted within it a witness—a people and a land where things were different. Through them, He would bring the Good News of His justice and lovingkindness to all the nations of the earth.

Our commission is the same. Unclouded fellowship with God, faithful exhortation of one another, beautiful Christian lives, all are not enough. There must be witness. The Church is likened to a golden lampstand, not an ornament. Nor is it enough that it should be of gold; it must shed forth the light of God into every corner of this dark world.

❧

NOVEMBER 18

"Therefore the sons are free. But, lest we cause them to
stumble . . . give unto them for me and thee."
Matthew 17:26, 27

God had never laid it down that His Son must
pay the Temple tax, and as Son of God there
was no necessity for Him to do anything whatever
about it. Indeed, we might feel that for Him to do
so would be to put Himself in the wrong position
of the "stranger" (verse 25). Then why did He do
it? "Lest we cause them to stumble."

Has it occurred to you that the very Son of
God himself uttered these words? There could of
course be no question at any time of his evading a duty; but that was not the point at issue
here. It was a question rather of His discarding
a privilege. This is the way of the cross, and the
principle is a significant and searching one. The
cross of Christ presents us with this expression
of God's will; namely, that like Him, we are required to forego what we might enjoy, in order
that others be not offended.

NOVEMBER 19

"For I determined not to know anything among you, save Jesus Christ, and him crucified. And I was with you in weakness, and in fear, and in much trembling."
I Corinthians 2:2, 3

The first of these statements applies to Paul's message, the second to his person. God requires that those who proclaim the message of the cross should have suffered the cross—should know themselves to be, in Paul's own words, crucified with Christ. We often think that when a person like Paul got up to speak, he must have felt confident in the strength of his own resources. But Paul's theme was Jesus Christ "crucified through weakness," and it was necessary, therefore, that he should tell it in conscious weakness himself.

We must allow God to cancel our self-sufficiency. When we confess before Him that we can do nothing in our own strength, then Christ will be able to manifest His power upon us. That which passes through the death of the cross and rises up again in life is of God, and being so will count mightily for Him.

NOVEMBER 20

"The world hated them, because they are not of the world, even as I am not of the world." John 17:14

From the standpoint of God's choice of us, we are "taken out of" the world; but from the standpoint of our new life, we are not of the world at all, but from above. As the people of God, heaven is not only our destiny, but our place of origin. This is an amazing thing, that in you and me there is an element that is essentially other-worldly. So other-worldly is it that no matter how this world may progress, that element in us can never become like it. The life we have as God's gift has no correspondence with the world, but is in perfect correspondence with heaven.

Though we may mingle with the world daily, it will never let us settle down and feel at home there. As soon as the world meets in us that which is of the divine nature, its hostility is at once aroused. This is not surprising, for let the world evolve how it will, it can never produce one Christian.

NOVEMBER 21

"Thus saith Jehovah, 'Make this valley full of trenches.'"
2 Kings 3:16

The history of Israel illustrates again and again how at any time man's unbelief can limit the omnipotence of God. Of course, man has no right to take what God has not given him, but how often do we find, rather, that what he takes possession of is but a fraction of what he might have had! It is a solemn fact that God's exercise of power can be limited by His people's unbelief.

On this occasion of the defeat of Mesha and the Moabites, the situation was otherwise. Faith prevailed and there was a wonderful display of divine power, but only because, in obedience to Elisha's instructions, men had got down to the monotonous task of digging. The trenches which His people prepared opened up the way for God to pour in His miracle-working power. Often, even today, the water of divine blessing finds its release through human channels.

NOVEMBER 22

"Now is my soul troubled; and what shall I say?"
John 12:27

The prayers of our Lord were always perfect prayers. Entering Jerusalem and facing the cross, he stopped to ask himself the questions, "What shall I say?" Jesus had no fear of death; yet at the same time He had His own feelings. He turned the matter over carefully and thought, "Shall I say, 'Father, save me from this hour?' No!" He could not pray that prayer, for He knew for what purpose He had arrived at that hour. So he prayed, "Father, glorify Thy name!" That prayer was answered immediately.

If our Lord, as Man on the earth and possessing the key to prayer, had in this deliberate way to set aside His own will and seek the will of God, how dare we, on the impulse of the moment, open our lips to utter words at random in our prayers to God? Let us ask ourselves, "What shall I say?" Then let us answer that question in terms consistent with the answer of Jesus. So shall we prove and experience the perfect will of God.

❧

NOVEMBER 23

"The cup that I drink ye shall drink; and with the baptism that I am baptized withal shall ye be baptized."
Mark 10:39

James and John longed to sit on either side of the Lord Jesus in His glory. Knowing, however, the inappropriateness of such a request, they dared not come out with it, but subtly suggested that He give them anything they might ask for. Jesus did not at once comply; instead He asked what they wanted. Their request carried two meanings: one a desire to be near the Lord, the other an ambition to wield more authority than the rest.

It was quite right for them to desire nearness to Christ, and He did not reject their desire. He simply assured them that to see it fulfilled they must drink His cup of suffering and be baptized with His baptism of death and resurrection. These two brothers did not know what they were asking, but neither did Jesus find fault with them for doing so. He did not even rebuke them personally for their ambitions, but replied that what they sought was not to be had for the asking. Nearness to Jesus in the future requires one condition only: nearness to Him now.

NOVEMBER 24

"Unto him that loveth us, and loosed us from our sins by his blood . . . to him be the glory and the dominion for ever and ever. Amen." Revelation 1:5, 6

Every time we are reminded of our redemption through the precious blood of Christ, our hearts well up with thanksgiving and praise. Indeed, that is all we can say, since in this matter there is no need to ask for anything; and in fact it would be unfitting to do so. We cannot invite the Lord to do what He has already done; we can only thank Him for it from our hearts.

Thanksgiving takes account of the Lord's work for us, but praise goes further. We praise Him for what He is. At the outset gratitude overwhelmed us, but as the novelty faded a little it left no vacuum; for we deal not with an event but with a Person, not with an action merely but with the Doer of it. Gradually the Lord Himself comes to fill our vision, and thanksgiving gives way to praise. "What a wonderful Savior," we cry, "is Jesus our Lord!"

NOVEMBER 25

"I will instruct thee and teach thee in the way which thou shalt go." Psalm 32:8

The horse and the mule can be made to obey their owner's will, though to realize his purpose he may have to use on them the bit and bridle and even the lash of the whip. God, however, never intended to direct His children in that kind of way. The horse and the mule "have no understanding," but His children can enjoy such an intimate relationship with Him that a mere hint of His wishes will suffice to bring a response from them.

Knowledge of the will of God is not so much a matter of finding the right method as of being the right man. If the man is not right with God, no method will avail to make that will clear to him. If the man is right, then the knowledge of God's will is a comparatively simple matter. This does not rule out methods, but we would emphasize that with the fullest knowledge of all the methods by which it may please God to make His will known, we shall remain in ignorance of it if we are not walking in quiet intimacy with Him.

NOVEMBER 26

*"And who is he that overcometh the world, but he that
believeth that Jesus is the Son of God?"* 1 John 5:5

You will discover that spiritual progress in
your life before God is invariably preceded
by dissatisfaction with your current condition.
All progress starts from dissatisfaction. You must
be pressed to a point where you feel that you have
come to an end, that a way out must be found.

Christ is our way out. Christ in us reacts on
our behalf to every kind of outside requirement.
When my temptation is pride, Christ will be my
humility if only I will make room for Him at
that hour. When passion is aroused, Christ will
express Himself as my patience. Every one of
life's daily demands is met by the many virtues
that spring from this one Life, and it is these
fresh discoveries of Christ in my hour of need
that mark my spiritual progress before God.

NOVEMBER 27

"Forsaking the right way, they went astray, having followed the way of Balaam." 2 Peter 2:15

Balaam was a prophet who worked for reward; he commercialized the prophetic ministry. He was not ignorant of the mind of God and was well aware that Israel was a people whom God would bless. Moreover, God had plainly forbidden him to comply with Balak's request and go and curse them. But the great reward lured him. How could he possibly obtain it? He decided that he would try to get God to reverse His decision.

The plan was carried into effect and at first seemed successful. God actually granted him the permission he had earlier refused. In fact, He simply let Balaam go his own self-chosen way, which according to the above verse was not "the right way" at all. How terrible to be released by God to go one's own greedy way instead of walking in the way of the Lord!

NOVEMBER 28

"Ourselves as your servants for Jesus' sake."
2 Corinthians 4:5

"We must remember that for Christ's sake we are the servants of others, and we should not only devote our time and strength to them, but also let our affections go out to them. God's demands of those who serve Him are very exacting. They allow us no leisure for self-occupation. If we cling to our pleasures and griefs, grudging to let go of our own interests, we shall be like a room that is too full of furniture to accommodate anything more.

To put it differently, we shall have expended all our emotions on ourselves and will have none to spare for others. We need to realize that there is a limit to our soul-strength, just as there is to the strength of our bodies. Our emotional powers are not boundless. If we exhaust our sympathies in one direction, we shall have none to give in another. Let us learn to enter into the feelings of others for the sake of Him who entered into ours.

≈

DECEMBER 1

"But I say unto you, Resist not him that is evil: but whosoever smiteth thee on thy right cheek, turn to him the other also." Matthew 5:39

What is taught us in the Sermon on the Mount? Is it not this—that within us, his sons, God has planted a new life; that that life makes upon us its own unique demands; and that in our conduct toward men we dare not be satisfied with anything less than what fulfills those demands. The Sermon does not tell us that provided we do what is right, then all is well. Men would protest, "Why present the other cheek? Surely it is enough if we accept the blow meekly without retaliating!" But God says otherwise. If when you are smitten on the one cheek, you do no more than bow your head and depart, you will find that the inner life will not be satisfied.

Many people tell us that the standards of Matthew 5–7 are too difficult; they are quite beyond us. I admit this. They are impossible. But here is the point: you have an inner life, and in a given situation that life gives you no rest until you do as the Sermon on the Mount requires. If the demands of his Son's life in you are met, God will take care of the consequences. We dare not stop short of His satisfaction.

❧

DECEMBER 2

"Let my prayer be set forth as incense before thee."
Psalm 141:2

True prayer comes from the desire of the heart, not from the imagination of the mind. It arises from a deep inner longing for the will of God. For this reason, the psalmist asked that his prayer might be offered to God as incense. All Old Testament incense came from the frankincense trees. To obtain it, successive incisions were made in the bark, and the tree then oozed a white resin from which the incense was manufactured. Hence prayer is not the offering of just anything that might be at hand; it is the presenting of something drawn painfully out of the innermost heart, as though it seeped from our very wounds.

How different is this from the easygoing prayers that we sometimes offer—prayers good to listen to, but all too empty of content! God answers these too, but let us remember well that our prayers are for God to hear, not for pleasing the ears of our fellow Christians. And God looks on the heart.

DECEMBER 3

"For where thy treasure is, there will thy heart be also."
Matthew 6:21

A brother once said to me, "My treasure is on earth, but my heart is in heaven." Such a brother should be exhibited in a Christian museum as a rarity! This is greater than a miracle, for it is something which the Lord said is quite impossible.

Mammon (or riches) is an idol which many have served over the past years and have found that such service gets a grip on the heart. The Lord's Word is both candid and sure: the heart always follows the treasure. There is no escape from this fact. No matter how one reasons, a man cannot serve both God and mammon. We must choose either one or the other.

DECEMBER 4

"Most gladly therefore will I rather glory in my weak-
nesses, that the power of Christ may rest upon me."
2 Corinthians 12:9

In this experience, the discipline of the Holy
Spirit leads Paul to a new discovery. He has
gone through a lot already, and he is not one
to fear danger or sickness; yet now he is being
sorely tried. The thorn in the flesh is no ordinary
thorn. If Paul says it is painful, then it must be
very painful indeed. He is weakened by it. But
at that very point God gives him grace which
he affirms is "sufficient." Paul has thus made a
dual discovery. He recognizes not merely God's
strength but also his own weaknesses—and is
not ashamed to tell us so.

Countless saints in the Church have been
carried through trial and testing by means of this
revelation of God to Paul. Oh, if we ourselves
only knew how weak we are! For as soon as weakness leaves us, power likewise departs. But like
Paul, the testings you and I go through perfect
the words we utter. As we then rise up and, ad-
mitting our own weakness, speak words that are
tempered through trial, our brothers and sisters,

themselves under testing, are given by God the grace and the strength to carry them through also.

❧

DECEMBER 5

"And Jacob vowed a vow, saying, If God will be with me, and will keep me in this way that I go . . . and Jehovah will be my God . . ." Genesis 28:20, 21

Now is it not true that you vowed a vow when you were first saved? Although you may have bargained with God while doing so, as Jacob did, your heart was right. As you set out upon His pathway, your desire toward Him was good.

But have you been like Jacob? The morning after, he put that vow behind his back. He traveled eastward and far from relying on God, he began at once to maneuver his way to success. He put his trust, not in the One whom he had asked to keep and clothe and feed him, but wholly in himself. How well he represents us! He looked to God, but he relied on his own cleverness. In Laban, however, God had prepared for this clever Jacob someone even cleverer. Step by step he was brought back by adversity to his vow, until at length he could only confess himself unworthy of the least of God's mercies.

❧

DECEMBER 6

"They washed their robes, and made them white in the blood of the Lamb." Revelation 7:14

We can only be made righteous by being cleansed through the blood. God offers us this way and no other. Not only our sins, but our behavior also must be cleansed. Not a single deed of any Christian is originally white. Even if we have some righteousness, it is mixed and not pure. Often we may have been outwardly kind to others, but were inwardly resentful. Often we have been patient with someone, only to go home and moan about him. Even after doing some righteous deed, therefore, we still need the cleansing of the blood.

So no Christian can ever weave himself a robe which is purely white. If he could make one that was 99 percent pure (and who can?), there would still be one percent of mixture. Even our good deeds, done out of love to the Lord, need the cleansing of the precious blood. But thus cleansed, we shall find ourselves arrayed in heavenly whiteness.

DECEMBER 7

"Surely the justice due to me is with Jehovah, and my recompense with my God." Isaiah 49:4

Our Lord Jesus is never discouraged. He was sent here to bring Jacob again to God, to gather Israel to Him; but with what result? He did not appear to have been successful. Indeed, by man's estimate, He was totally defeated, for Jacob did not return to God. Israel did not accept Him. Instead, the Jews rejected Jesus and slew Him as a criminal.

Had we to live on earth rejected by men and apparently fruitless in service, it is more than likely that we should become aggrieved and cry out for justice. Not so the Lord. He had committed Himself to the Father, and neither gain nor loss was able to touch Him. He was careful about one thing only: to leave the vindication and the reward to the Father. If our justice is safe with God, our recompense from Him is also sure.

DECEMBER 8

"Let all bitterness, and wrath, and anger . . . be put away from you." Ephesians 4:31

I am a Christian, and I feel an outburst of temper rising within me. I cannot repress it by merely repeating such Scriptures as "My old man was crucified with Christ," "I have died to sin," for afterwards I have to admit that if I were really dead I could not have lost my temper anyway! No, the simple recital of Bible words produces no result.

The cross of Christ is not meant to relieve our symptoms, but rather to deal with our disease. The disease which causes the temper has to do with our "self." Let no one excuse himself by saying that it is his disposition to be quick-tempered, for the slow can equally lose his temper, though he may manifest it in a different way. We need to know how to deny our self. This is where the death of Christ is effective. If self is being dealt with before God, then our explosive ill temper will naturally fade away.

DECEMBER 9

"But whosoever drinketh of the water that I shall give him shall never thirst." John 4:14

The Lord Jesus gives people permanent satisfaction. Why then are we so often unsatisfied? Why is there yet a craving within us for something else? We are attentive enough to the promise of this verse, but have we overlooked the declaration which preceded it? Pointing to the well of Sychar, Jesus had said, "Every one that drinketh of this water shall thirst again." It is "this water" that has reawakened our cravings and that fails to satisfy them.

It never will. Our mistake is to build our hopes—even Christian hopes—on the fleeting things of time. That explains the disappointment. The first clause, "shall thirst again," was necessary to drive us to the second, "shall never thirst." We, whom the Lord intends to satisfy fully, often need reminding not to drink from other sources.

◆

DECEMBER 10

"And Enoch walked with God after he begat Methuselah." Genesis 5:22

We do not know anything about Enoch before he was sixty-five years old, but after he begat Methuselah we discover something special: we learn that he walked with God for 300 years before he was taken up. This is very significant. When the burden of having a family came upon Enoch, he became aware of his unfitness. He felt the responsibility heavy on him, so he came near to God.

The record does not say that he walked with God only when Methuselah was born, but that he individually maintained this personal association as though convinced that unless he was intimate with God, he could not lead his son. Nor does it say that children distracted him from his course. He begat many sons and daughters during those three centuries, but all the while he continued to walk with God. Parenthood itself should not hinder people from this walk of faith; rather, since the bearing of family responsibilities reveals one's true spiritual state, should it constrain them so to walk. And when the pilgrimage was completed, Enoch was not; for God took him.

DECEMBER 11

"For to you is the promise, and to your children."
Acts 2:39

The biblical view of children is always that they are God's gift to us. They are ours on trust from Him. You cannot say, "This child is mine," as if he were exclusively yours, giving you unlimited rights over him until he becomes a man. Such a concept is heathen, not Christian. Christianity never recognizes one's children as one's private property. They are a divine trust, to be held for the Giver.

From the first God sees the child as a person with his own rights and privileges. He does not deny the child's self-respect, nor violate his freedom, nor erase his independent personality when he places him in your hand. He trusts you with him for his good and yours. I would tell parents to be slow in demanding strict obedience from their children, and ask them first to set themselves to be good parents before the Lord.

❧

DECEMBER 12

"The things which are impossible with men are possible with God." Luke 18:27

Jesus has just stated that if it is absolutely impossible for a camel to pass through a needle's eye, then it is even more impossible for a rich man to enter into the kingdom of God. We Christians are all like camels; big or small ones, maybe, but still camels. So when Peter heard this statement, he was uneasy. If eternal life is to be obtained by such impossible contortions, then who can be saved? Have we all to set to work to impoverish ourselves before we are saved?

The Lord Jesus answered Peter's problem with one sentence: "The things which are impossible with men are possible with God." What was wrong with the young ruler was not his wealth so much as the fact that he went away sorrowful. Why did he not cry out for grace? Why did he not ask God to do the impossible for him? Man's failure is not due to his weakness, but to his unwillingness to let God deliver him.

DECEMBER 13

"Let him kiss me with the kisses of his mouth; for thy love is better than wine." Song of Songs 1:2

A kiss is an act of personal, wholehearted committal. It means that all the attention is centered on the one person. (No one kisses two persons at the same time!) Of course there can always be the hypocritical kiss of a Judas, or the merely formal salutation which Simon the Pharisee failed to give to Jesus; but these have no place here, for the words are spoken by one whose heart has been captivated by the Lord and who forgets everybody else in the act of devotion which makes everything of Him.

Such a one longs for the closest communion with God. The Father's kiss of forgiveness was sweet, but this is something more. It is the Lord's response to an outgoing of devotion from one who finds His love better than all else.

DECEMBER 14

"But let him ask in faith, nothing doubting." James 1:6

I once had a Christian friend who was in urgent need of $150. At that time we lived in a riverside village where no ferryboat operated on Saturdays or Sundays. It was already Saturday and he needed the money for the following Monday. He prayed to God and became assured that the money would come to him on the Monday. As he went out to preach the gospel, he met his window-cleaner who reminded him that he owed him a dollar for work done; so he paid him from the remaining two dollars which he had in his pocket. Going on further he met a beggar who asked for alms. His remaining dollar seemed very precious to him, but he felt that he must give it all to the beggar.

As his last dollar went out, God came in. He became exceedingly happy, having nothing now to depend on but God alone. He returned home and slept peacefully. On the Lord's day he was occupied as usual in his service. Monday came, and sure enough $150 arrived by telegram, even though this means of remittance was very costly. God may not be early, but He is never late! Only He is always right on time.

DECEMBER 15

Tony man willeth to do his will, he shall know of the teaching, whether it is of God, or whether I speak from myself." John 7:17

God grants us light to the degree that He sees we genuinely desire to know His will and do it. A heart that is hardened or self-seeking or self-reliant may shut out God's light. If we truly want Him to illumine us, we must be tender, unselfish, dependent on Him.

In short, we must be humble, for we are subject to error. What we judge as right may not necessarily be right; what we judge as wrong may not be wrong at all. We may see darkness as light, or see light and think it darkness. It is so easy for us to act overconfidently and in haste on these mistaken grounds. It is only the light of God that can show us the true character of a thing. Let us ask for that light out of a pure desire for His will, for the Christian life should not be filled with problems, doubts, hesitations, and mistakes.

DECEMBER 16

*"How should one chase a thousand, and two put ten
thousand to flight . ." Deuteronomy 32:30*

Christianity is unique in that it is not only individual but corporate in nature. It stresses
the coming together of the saints. Other religions
advocate piety; Christianity alone calls people to
assemble.

It is promised here that whereas one chases
off 1,000 foes, two put to flight ten times that
number. We do not know how this is possible,
for the arithmetic seems wrong, but it is a fact.
We would calculate that if one can chase 1,000,
then two will dispose of 2,000. But God says No.

Eight thousand more will flee when two of
His children unite. This added effectiveness is
the surplus gained from meeting and working
together. Let us not, therefore, be content with
personal grace alone. God has so much more He
can do with us together.

DECEMBER 17

"In that he saith, A new covenant, he hath made the first old. But that which is becoming old and waxeth aged is nigh unto vanishing away." Hebrews 8:13

In Acts 21 Paul went into the Temple to perform a vow. Let us not hastily conclude that he was wrong to do so. We dare not apply God's ultimate standards to His saints in every age, since His movement toward the final goal is progressive. What is required of you and me today is not that we attain to God's ultimate, but that we keep in step with Him now. At that period of his life, it may have been perfectly right for Paul to purify himself in the Temple in accordance with the Old Covenant, but what was fitting then could have been wrong at a later time.

From beginning to end, the book of the Acts is a progressive narrative. Even when the record closes with chapter 28, the movement of the Spirit does not cease. The tide flows on throughout succeeding generations, and all the while God keeps raising up those who will make their specific contribution to each stage of His onward move.

DECEMBER 18

"And she said, thy handmaid hath not any thing in the house, save a pot of oil." 2 Kings 4:2

The work of the Holy Spirit is not "once empty, always full"; it is "keeping on being empty to keep on being full." The woman's difficulty was having too few vessels. She was told to borrow "not a few," which is to say "the more the better." The greater the space, the greater will be the fullness. This is the rule which God wants us to learn.

He waits for us to be empty. If you have an unlimited vacancy, the Holy Spirit will occupy it all, dispensing to you His unlimited fullness. Let me repeat: our emptying needs to be continuous. To the degree that we empty ourselves, God can fill us. The emptying is our responsibility, just as the filling is His. God wants to see the hungry filled with good things. Only those who presume to be rich will He send away empty.

DECEMBER 19

"Let us cleanse ourselves from all defilement of flesh and spirit, perfecting holiness in the fear of God."
2 Corinthians 7:1

We never cease to need God's cleansing of our spirits. As His children, we come often face to face with the cross of Christ and it never confronts us in vain. Each time some new defect in us is brought to light and dealt with, often painfully, and we are cleansed once again and our spirits are purified.

If the Spirit of the Lord were to reject every man who had some defect, things would be much simpler. It would be easy to draw a clear line between what is the work of the flesh and what of the Spirit. The problem is compounded, however, because God does not reject us outright, even though our spirit is not pure and our flesh may be active. Instead He uses us, and next time deals with us afresh by His cross. Although He uses us, let us be careful that we never lose sight of our own impurity. And the more He uses us, the more willingly let us subject ourselves again to His cleansing work.

DECEMBER 20

"I have heard thy prayer, I have seen thy tears."
2 Kings 20:5

How good it is to know that God sees our tears. As Hezekiah prayed, he also wept; and God answered him. Such tearful prayers can move God's heart. It seems that whatever cannot move your heart cannot move God's heart either. A weeping before men may reveal your weakness and lack of manly strength, but a weeping before God is different.

Yet be clear about this, that tears are futile if they are not shed before God. There are people who are prone to weeping, but if a man's cry simply expresses his own sorrow and distress, it will not produce any positive results. Tears accompanied by prayer, however, are effective. Every time you cry in distress, why not therefore add prayer? The supplications of the Lord Jesus went up to God with strong crying and tears, and He was heard because He feared.

DECEMBER 21

"But I have this against thee, that thou didst leave thy first love." Revelation 2:4

The expression "first love" refers not only to primacy in time, but also in quality. The story of the prodigal son's return home tells us that the father called for "the best robe" to be brought to replace the penitent's rags. This is the same word. The first love is the best love.

The tragedy in this church at Ephesus was that it had left or moved away from that devotion which gave the Lord the first place in their affections. There was, however, a hope. It is not always possible to recover what has been lost, but it is always open to us to return to a position from which we have strayed. The Lord calls each of us who has wandered to come back to the experience of loving him best, to return to our first love.

DECEMBER 22

"Having confessed that they were strangers and pilgrims on the earth." Hebrews 11:13

What does it mean to be a stranger and a pilgrim? Let me use an illustration. During my stay in England, shortly before the Munich crisis, I noticed people preparing for war by digging trenches, preparing shelters, and distributing masks for poisonous gas. My feelings at that time were entirely different from those of the Englishmen. I watched them prepare for war until the news came that a pact had been signed. Many could not sleep that night. They sang and they shouted.

But what was my reaction? I watched unmoved. While they had been busily preparing for war, I had watched coldly; now when they rejoiced over peace, I still watched coldly. I was a sojourner. I would soon go away. In their joy and in their sorrow I was merely an observer. So it was that I realized what it means to be an alien. My attitude toward England was neutral. I hoped for her good; I wished her peace; but my interests lay elsewhere.

DECEMBER 23

"Thou art fair, O my love, as Tirzah, comely as Jerusa-
lem, terrible as an army with banners."
Song of Songs 6:4

I t is in the heavenly realm that the saints have
their union with Christ, but there too they
meet the real force of the enemy's attacks. God
never intended believers to possess heavenly
beauty merely and be without the spiritual stam-
ina to fight His battles. Unfurled banners denote
victory. It is the defeated who have to roll them
up. Christ's beloved people are meant to make
an impact in the heavens, marching on triumphantly as an army.

Yet when that is said, they are at the same
time likened to Tirzah, a place renowned for its
beauty, and are described as being comely as Jerusalem, the city of God. There is no contradic-
tion here. The Church which is beautiful to God
will be a challenge to His enemies.

DECEMBER 24

"For we have not a high priest that cannot be touched with the feeling of our infirmities." Hebrews 4:15

Why was it that our Lord Jesus did not enter this world as a grown man? Why did He have to be conceived as a baby, to be nursed and carried, until He gradually grew up to manhood? Why was He obliged to pass through more than thirty years of earthly sufferings? Could He not as easily have accomplished the work of redemption by coming down into the world and being crucified three days later? The answer is that He suffered chastening and hardship and frustration and disappointment in order that He might be sympathetic with you and me.

Sympathy is compassion, "suffering together." He feels with you. He is always sympathetic toward your infirmities, never to the sins you commit, but always to the sufferings of your body and distresses of your soul. He has been through it all. He not only has the grace to save you; He also has the heart to sympathize with you.

DECEMBER 25

"They shall call his name Immanuel; which is, being interpreted, God with us." Matthew 1:23

The whole outworking of redemption activities was initiated by this coming of the Babe to Bethlehem. It illustrates in a supreme way the quiet and apparently small character of God's beginnings. Only a few humble shepherds were called in to witness this unique addition to the human race by which the eternal Son of God was thereafter able to claim to be the Son of Man. Jesus himself adopted this description of Himself and seemed to delight in it. Though truly God, He was now truly Man.

The title of Immanuel was never fully understood while Jesus was on earth and was probably never used by those nearest to Him. Since Calvary and Pentecost, however, believers have claimed it as one of the most precious of His many names. He set His own seal on it when He assured His adoring apostles, "Lo, I am with you alway." Since He added "unto the end of the age," we too can claim Him as our ever-present Immanuel.

~

DECEMBER 26

"And the peace of God, which passeth all understanding, shall guard your hearts and your thoughts in Christ Jesus." Philippians 4:7

" The peace of God" is not just a certain kind of peace that God bestows upon us. It is God's own peace, the very peace which is inherent in His nature. His is a peace that nothing can disturb. When He created the angels, and when rebellion broke out in their ranks with far-reaching effects in His universe, not even so dark a calamity could disturb Him. He proceeded to realize His heart's desire by repairing the damage done on the earth and then creating another order of beings—man.

Then man too fell. Yet the peace of God remained undisturbed. We would have expected Him to act immediately to make good the damage; but not so. God could wait for "the fullness of time" before sending His Son to recover what was lost. A wait of thousands of years put no strain on His peace. God promises that a peace of this quality will guard the hearts and thoughts of those who fulfill His condition of commiting everything to Him in prayer.

ᕈ

DECEMBER 27

"And if any man sin, we have an Advocate with the Father." 1 John 2:1

What the Lord has done is wholly to forgive us for our sins and totally to cleanse us from all unrighteousness. When Scripture says "all," there is no doubt that God means all. Let us not divide His Word. He forgives all our sins, not only of the past but right up to date—sins that we are conscious of as well as those of which we are unaware.

"If any man sin." God has spoken to us that we should not sin. Faced with His great forgiveness, our gratitude, far from making us careless, will surely constrain us not to sin. But if a Christian should sin, he has an Advocate with the Father, Jesus Christ the righteous. It is now a family affair, as the words "with the Father" indicate. The very fact that the Son intercedes for us there guarantees that the least believer, however lately entered upon the Father-Son relationship with God has unqualified forgiveness.

DECEMBER 28

"And not one of them said that aught of the things which he possessed was his own; but they had all things common." Acts 4:32

Once these men had gained eternal life, their possessions began to lose their grip on them, and in quite a natural way they disposed of their properties. Applying this to us who come to follow the Lord today, should it not be quite natural to us that our many possessions are placed at His disposal?

From my own personal life may I tell you something which may make you laugh. For nearly twenty years I have had the habit of purchasing a half dozen or so of anything I buy for myself. For example, if I buy a safety razor blade, I purchase a dozen of them, to avoid buying for my own self alone. Of course I cannot give a razor blade to each of a thousand or more brethren, but if I give to other brothers before I use my own, it saves me from feeling in a wrong way that the razor belongs exclusively to me. This has proved to be one small way of holding my material possessions for God.

❧

DECEMBER 29

"Speak unto the children of Israel, that they bring thee
a red heifer without spot, wherein is no blemish, and
upon which never came yoke." Numbers 19:2

While all Israel's other sacrifices were offered to meet current needs, the red heifer alone was different. It was offered to provide for future eventualities. The whole heifer was to be burned. Then the ashes were collected and stored, so that as the need arose they could be mixed with running water and sprinkled on an unclean person to make him clean.

In those ashes was embodied all the efficacy of redemption. Whenever a man was defiled, he had no need to slay another heifer; he needed only to be sprinkled with this water. Putting this in Christian terms, a believer today does not need the Lord Jesus to work for him a second time; he has the incorruptible ashes and living water of Christ's finished work for his cleansing. The atonement which God has wrought for us in Christ is always at once available for our need.

DECEMBER 30

"And I will restore to you the years that the locust hath eaten." Joel 2:25

Do our hearts ache over the years we have foolishly squandered? Then let us thank God for the comfort of knowing His power to restore them. "Alas," we lament, "our best years have been devoured by the locusts. They are lost now never to be regained. What shall we do?" The answer is, "Nothing!" It is God who will restore those years. As to the time wasted, a lost decade of ours may have been worth no more than one day in God's eyes; but if hereafter we redeem the time by using it for God, then one day may become equal in value to 1,000 years.

For the day on earth is not clocked in heaven on the basis of twenty-four hours. Instead, God has His own moral scale of computation. If our service is according to His will, let us take courage. Who can tell what a single hour may count for in His sight?

DECEMBER 31

"Among whom ye are seen as lights in the world."
Philippians 2:15

A candle should burn until it is all consumed; likewise a man's testimony should continue until his death. If one candle's light is to live on, then it needs to kindle another before it is completely burned out. By kindling candle after candle, the light can shine on and on until it covers the whole world. Such is the testimony of the Church.

When the Son of God came to the earth, He kindled a few candles; later on He ignited another candle in Paul, and of course many more. During the 2,000 years since then, the Church's light continued burning on in candle after candle. Many have even sacrificed their lives to ignite others, but although the first candle gutters out, the second one continues, and so on and so on. Go therefore and witness for the Lord! Let His testimony shine out in the earth unceasingly.

INDEX TO SCRIPTURES

John: (continued)

Acts:

Acts: (continued)

Romans:

1 Corinthians:

Philippians: (continued)

    4:7 .... Dec. 26
    4:8 ....June 28
    4:11 ....June 7
    4:13 .... Sept. 27
    4:19 .... Aug. 4

Colossians:

    1:24 ....July 20
    1:27 .... Feb. 12
    2:15 ....May 1
    2:19 ....Sept. 15
    3:4 .... Mar. 1
    3:11 ....July 10
    3:21 ....July 26

1 Thessalonians:

    1:9, 10 .... Sept. 4

2 Thessalonians:

    2:11 .... Mar. 27

1 Timothy:

    1:12 .... Aug. 8
    1:15 .... Mar. 14
    1:19 .... Mar. 7
    5:13 ....April 1
    6:12 .... Feb. 24

2 Timothy:

    1:8 ....Jan. 26
    3:15 ....July 8
    3:16, 17 ....Oct. 31
    4:6, 7 ....Oct. 8

Hebrews:

    4:15 .... Dec. 24
    5:8 .... Feb. 26

Hebrews: (continued)

    6:1 .... Aug. 31
    7:25 ....Jan. 13
    8:13 .... Dec. 17
    9:14 ....Jan. 21
    11:8 ....Oct. 15
    11:13 .... Dec. 22
    12:4 ....June 5
    12:9 .... Sept. 3
    13:1 ....Oct. 9
    13:8 ....April 20
    13:15 ....Sept. 6

James:

    1:6 .... Dec. 14
    1:22 .... Mar. 18
    2:5 ....Oct. 28
    4:4 ....May 30
    4:7 ....May 28
    5:14, 15 ....July 30
    5:18 ....May 6

1 Peter:

    2:5 ....Jan. 28
    2:6 .... Sept. 12
    2:17 ....Oct. 10
    2:24 ....May 16
    3:5 .... Aug. 18
    3:7 ....July 22
    4:19 ....July 21

2 Peter:

    1:5 ....Oct. 29
    1:20 ....May 4
    1:21 .... Aug. 27
    2:15 .... Nov. 27

This book was produced by CLC Publications. We hope it has been life-changing and has given you a fresh experience of God through the work of the Holy Spirit. CLC Publications is an outreach of CLC Ministries International, a global literature mission with work in over 50 countries. If you would like to know more about us or are interested in opportunities to serve with a faith mission, we invite you to contact us at:

CLC Ministries International
P.O. Box 1449
Fort Washington, PA 19034

———————

Phone: (215) 542-1242
E-mail: orders@clcpublications.com
Website: www.clcpublications.com

DO YOU LOVE GOOD CHRISTIAN BOOKS?
Do you have a heart for worldwide missions?

You can receive a FREE subscription to
CLC's newsletter on global literature missions
Order by e-mail at:

clcworld@clcusa.org

Or fill in the coupon below and mail to:

P.O. Box 1449
Fort Washington, PA 19034

FREE *CLCWORLD* SUBSCRIPTION!

Name: _____

Address:_____

_____

Phone: _____ **Email:**_____

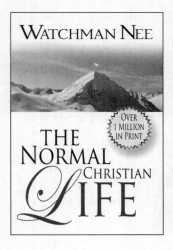

Starting from key passages in Romans, Nee reveals the secret of spiritual vitality that should be the normal experience of every Christian.

Trade Paper
Size 5 ¼ x 8, Pages 255
ISBN 978-0-87508-990-4
$11.99

An inspiring look at Ephesians, opening our eyes to the process of Christian living and maturity.

Trade Paper
Size 5 ¼ x 8, Pages 96
ISBN 978-0-87508-973-7
$8.99

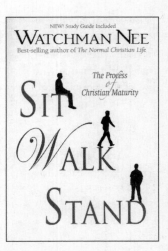

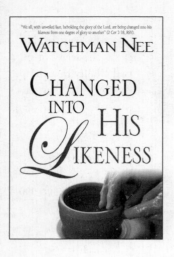

This book makes a valuable contribution to an understanding of God's way with His own people, through a study of the lives of Abraham, Isaac and Jacob.

Trade Paper
Size 5 ¼ x 8, Pages 90
ISBN 978-0-87508-859-4
$9.99

Nee states that despite Satan's influence over worldly things, Christians must learn how to live in the world but not of it.

Trade Paper
Size 5 ¼ x 8, Pages 135
ISBN 978-0-87508-787-0
$8.99

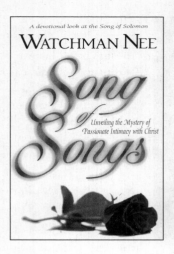

Watchman Nee explores
the principles found
in the book of Song of
Songs, as it portrays
the love relationship
between God and the
individual believer.

Trade Paper
Size 5 ¼ x 8, Pages 231
ISBN 978-0-87508-851-8
$10.99

From the writings of
Watchman Nee, here
are daily devotional me-
diations and Scripture
passages to refresh your
thoughts on God.

Trade Paper
Size 5 ¼ x 8, Pages 221
ISBN 978-0-87508-699-6
$11.99

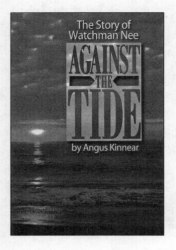
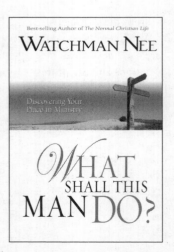